The Promise of Surfing Rainbows

Opening your energy flow attracts a treasured life...

Written by P.D.M. Dolce

BALBOA
PRESS

Playing with infinite potential for unlimited possibilities

Balboa Press books may be ordered through booksellers or by contacting:

Balboa Press
A Division of Hay House
1663 Liberty Drive
Bloomington, IN 47403
www.balboapress.com
1-(877) 407-4847

ISBN: 978-1-4525-0021-8 (sc)
ISBN: 978-1-4525-0029-4 (e)

Library of Congress Control Number: 2010914337

Printed in the United States of America

Balboa Press rev. date: 9/24/2010

ii

Acknowledgments

We are grateful to all who have loved and supported us during the years we have been creating our project, Surfing Rainbows. It's been a great journey during which two babies were rainbow surfed into existence, friends were healed, businesses achieved success and everyone connected with this endeavor enjoyed happier, healthier lives.

We wish to acknowledge all of those whose ideas have in some way contributed to what has become Surfing Rainbows. In addition to the many authors cited in the book, we offer our thanks to Og Mandino, Abraham-Hicks, Neale Donald Walsch, Robert Evans, Louise Hay and Adam J. Jackson.

Our thanks go also to Gemma Farrell of Accelerator Books for her many contributions and especially for her patience.

Contents

Introduction

If some area of your life is not as good as you would like it to be, let *The Promise of Surfing Rainbows* offer you a way of overcoming any issue that you might be facing. This book holds a promise that it will give you the tools that can take you to a life that you will truly love living.

These powerful tools come primarily from two sources – science and ancient wisdom. Quantum physics has provided us with a new understanding of how our energy affects our surroundings. Ironically, this knowledge is not new at all. It was part of the ancient wisdom that was almost lost over the years.

Once scientists and philosophers realized that this world of ours is so much more than the physical and that there is a creative energy available to everyone, the door opened to a new modern awareness of the knowledge that is centuries old.

Surfing Rainbows takes a deep look at these concepts as well as a fresh look at the ancient wisdom itself to reveal the crucial link to creating and achieving all that we desire. *The Promise of Surfing Rainbows* completes a picture that has only been presented in part before. The crucial link that is revealed is the link between the commonly understood term called the Law of Attraction and the practice of Energy Alignment through chakra balancing, which is at the core of all widely accepted holistic therapies.

The significance of the crucial link between the Law of Attraction and Energy Alignment is that separately these concepts have already improved the lives of millions, but when combined they provide the simplest way of ensuring that you successfully achieve your desires.

As soon as the significance of the crucial link is appreciated, there will be an enormous "aha" moment, followed by a lifetime of greater happiness. This may seem like a very farfetched claim. However, when this one powerful idea is understood, it will seem obvious. Sometimes it is the most obvious things that are the most life changing.

If the term "Surfing Rainbows" seems too lighthearted for such a life-changing endeavor, there is a simple explanation. The seven colours of the chakras are the same seven colours of the rainbow, and the act of surfing implies a fun, easy and effortless flow of energy to arrive at a desired destination. To give some reassurance about how "Surfing Rainbows" can help you achieve your own desires, there are many endorsements by inspiring people within the pages of this book, and there are many testimonials on the website.

You really have nothing to lose and absolutely everything to gain as you start Surfing Rainbows to enjoy the best life has to offer. The time-proven concepts upon which this is based give you the results.

Let life's adventures begin...

Part One
What is
Surfing Rainbows?

Chapter 1

Surfing Rainbows Completes the Picture

The Chakras and Their Connection to the Law of Attraction

There have been many good books published on the Law of Attraction, and just as many published about the energy centres in the body known as chakras. Surfing Rainbows takes both of these ancient concepts, combines their wisdom and reveals in-depth how they are fundamentally connected.

This connection is fabulously exciting because it revolutionizes how to achieve a healthy, happy successful life, regardless of your race, religion, education, background or current circumstances.

Basically, when your chakras are more in balance, there is more positive energy flowing through you and you can therefore benefit more fully from the Law of Attraction. That benefit to you is the fulfillment of your desires. If you are unfamiliar with these concepts then it may all sound rather complex but actually it is magnificently simple as this book aims to explain.

Surfing Rainbows

You may wish to enjoy better health, greater wealth or a happier life. You may want to change your job, enjoy a better relationship, buy a new home, gain weight or slim down. You may not know how to achieve this, but Surfing Rainbows can be applied to any area of your life that you would like to improve, so that your life begins to "flow" and your desires are more easily realized.

Even if others tell you that your desires are impossible, remember, there is a first time for everything. Years ago it was considered impossible to walk on the moon, to have water running from a tap, or to have light come on at the flick of a switch. What was once thought of as impossible is now commonplace. Just look at the number of people who have recovered from diseases that in the past were considered incurable!

If you have many desires and you are not sure where to start, it may seem too overwhelming to address them all at once. In that case, use this book for one desire at a time and as each desire is realized, it will give you more confidence about achieving your next one. This is a book to read, use and reuse. It was written with the aim of becoming your friend and helpful guide.

Chapter 2

Two Time-Proven Principles

Although you do not need to understand much about chakras or the Law of Attraction to benefit from Surfing Rainbows, an overview is given now for those who may like to find out more about them.

The Chakras

The intention of holistic medicine is to align the body's energy flow. At the core of this energy flow are the body's energy centres known as chakras.

When you feel bad, your energy is out of alignment and not fully flowing. When you feel good, your energy is more in alignment and your energy is flowing more fully.

We cannot see our energy and we cannot see these energy centres. Ancient cultures discovered that the energy centres comprise spinning vortices that spin in a way that is similar to other fluid vortices such as whirlpools, waterspouts and hurricanes, all of which draw energy into themselves. The body has many chakras but there are seven major ones, situated in a straight vertical line correlating to the spine, through the centre of the body. The first of these major chakras extends downwards from the base of the spine, while the seventh chakra extends vertically upwards at the top of the head. Each of the other five chakras have front and rear spinning vortices, which affects the energy that is drawn into that part of the body as shown on the following illustration.

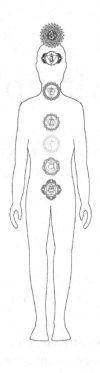
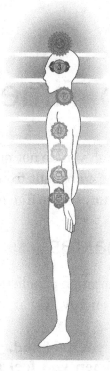

7th Chakra (purple)

6th Chakra (indigo)

5th Chakra (blue)

4th Chakra (green)

3rd Chakra (yellow)

2nd Chakra (orange)

1st Chakra (red)

The Seven Major Chakras
© Sentir 2009

The existence of chakras has been validated by Western science. Dr. Valerie Hunt[1] used EMG electrodes (similar to those used to record astronauts' brain, heart and muscle signals in space) to identify new dynamic tension patterns that are unlike any of the other bodily tension systems. These patterns correspond to the chakra positions documented centuries ago by ancient cultures.

The bioelectrical energy variations in the areas of skin that correspond to the positions of the chakras were shown to lie within the band of vibration frequencies 1,000 and 1,600 cycles per second, whereas the normal vibrational frequency of brain waves is between 0 and 100 cycles per second.

Since each chakra energy centre has a different number of vortices, they resonate at a different vibrational frequency, and as colour is simply a frequency of energy, the chakras are therefore associated with different colours. The lower

---

1   Dr. V. Hunt, *Infinite Mind, The Science of Human Vibrations (Malibu Publishing, 1995).*

vibrational frequencies of colour relate to the lower numbered chakras, and the seventh chakra resonates with the colour of highest vibrational frequency.

Western scientists have mathematically analyzed the recorded wave patterns of the chakras and have seen consistent waveforms and frequencies that correlate to the colours of the rainbow as documented by the ancient cultures.

It is accepted from ancient principles that the functioning of the chakras is affected by how we think and feel. Scientific studies have also shown that thoughts produce chemical impulses called peptides, which are the brain's system of communicating with the body in an effort to maintain good health and include a so-called "feel good" endorphin. Scientists have discovered that the largest clumps of peptide receptors are concentrated in the locations corresponding to the chakras.[2]

Each of the seven major chakras is also associated with a nerve plexus, endocrine gland, lymphatic system and various organs. More detail on which chakra relates to which nerve plexus, endocrine gland, etc. is given later in this book. The chemical hormones secreted by the endocrine glands have a dramatic effect on their associated parts of the body, as do the nerve transmissions within the brain, spinal cord and peripheral nerves. This explains how the chakras are therefore also linked with particular parts of the body.

When we feel off-colour, our chakra energy centres are out of balance. If this continues over time, ill health results in the associated part of the body that is linked to the relevant endocrine gland, nerve plexus or organ. Indeed, Dr. Harold Saxton Burr[3], a Neuroanatomist from Yale University, used an ordinary voltmeter to measure the changes in energy when the body is unwell, and found a major difference in those who are well and those who are sick.

When the chakras are in balance and drawing positive energy inwards, good health is the result and we feel more vibrant with higher energy levels. The relevance of this will become evident as we move on to explore the Law of Attraction.

---

2   Dr. Candace Pert, Molecules of Emotion: Why You Feel The Way You Feel (Simon & Shuster,1997)
3   Dr Harold S Burr, *The Fields of Life: Our Links to the Universe* (New York, Ballantine Books,1972)

The Law of Attraction

New insights from quantum physics are changing and clarifying our current understanding of our world, thereby helping us expand our minds to embrace new opportunities.

"For the last four hundred years, an unstated assumption of science is that human intention cannot affect what we call 'physical reality.'
Our experimental research of the past decade shows that, for today's world and under the right conditions, this assumption is no longer correct.
We humans are much more than we think we are and Psychoenergetic Science continues to expand the proof of it."
—William A. Tiller, Ph.D.

Quantum physics is a relatively new area of science and its application is responsible for various technical advances, including lasers, mobile phones, televisions and computers. Examples of the application of this technology within Western medicine include CT Scans and the firing of a wave frequency to clear kidney stones.

Modern quantum physics states that we are part of one large energy field and we are simply a mass of energy, physical atoms comprising energy vortices that are constantly vibrating and spinning.

Moving energy causes vibrations at different frequencies. If the radio in your car is on at full blast, in addition to hearing the sound, you will also see and feel the speakers vibrating. The colours you see are vibrations of different frequencies and wavelengths. These hit the retina at the back of the eye and are interpreted by the brain as coloured images.

The same is true of smell. The brain interprets the vibrations that hit the receptors in your nose as varying ranges of odour. Again, the same principle applies with your sense of taste as picked up by the receptors on your tongue. Your vocal cords make vibrations to give you your words, and your muscle movements and nerve impulses give constant vibrations to produce your actions.

The thoughts that produce positive emotions vibrate at a different speed than the thoughts that produce negative emotions. As you change your thoughts, you change the frequency of your energy waves, which in turn change your feelings. Quantum physicists are now able to measure these different vibrations.

To understand the importance of this, consider a walky-talky (two-way radio). If you want to connect with someone using a walky-talky, you have to be on the same wavelength to be able to make contact. And if you want to communicate with someone else on a different frequency, then you have to change the channel on the walky-talky so that you can make contact by sending and receiving on that new wavelength.

Similarly, our energy is vibrating constantly and so we are sending out vibrations (vibes) corresponding to our feelings all the time. What we are saying, thinking or doing affects how we feel, and creates our vibe. To understand how the frequency of the vibes we send out depends on our thoughts and feelings, consider what would happen if you met someone who was depressed and another who was excited; no matter what they said about how they feel, you would instinctively pick up on their vibes.

The Law of Attraction states that the vibes we send out attract the vibrations of the same frequency back, and that is what determines whether or not we are able to connect with and receive our desires. An example of "like vibrations attracting like vibrations" is the tuning fork. If there are many different tuning forks in the same room and one is "pinged," all the other tuning forks will remain quiet except the one that is calibrated to the same vibrational pitch. That one will pick up the sound vibration of the "pinged" fork and chime in with its own sound.

You always gravitate towards situations, events and people that resonate on your own wavelength. Sometimes the correlation is obvious. For example, if you shout at someone, it is likely you will get an angry or defensive response back. The worse you feel, the worse things may seem to become. A grimace may slam doors shut, whereas smiles open them.

Whatever you focus your attention on through your thoughts, words and actions impacts the vibes you send out and consequently what you attract back.

That is why you are drawn to what you focus your attention on, whether they are the things you want or the things you do not want.

Consider a situation where a man is desperate for a partner. If he wants a long-term, loving relationship that would make him really happy, he will not be able to attract it while he remains desperate, because he is on the wrong wavelength to be able to receive love, however much he wants it.

To attract something that would make you happy, the vibes you send and receive have to match. They have to be on the same wavelength; otherwise rather than attracting your desire you are repelling it.

To use the example of the walky-talky: when you want to communicate with someone on a different wavelength using a walky-talky, you have to change the frequency on which it sends and receives. Likewise, if you want to be able to change the circumstances you are experiencing, you must change the frequency you are sending out through your vibes. You can do this by changing the thoughts that affect your feelings, vibes and your frequency. As you change your own frequencies, you broadcast different vibes and attract back different circumstances.

Our feelings give us instant, accurate feedback about what frequency we are broadcasting on and therefore they give us a clear indication of whether we are going to like what we are attracting back.

When you have positive thoughts, they generate positive feelings and attract more positive life experiences back to you. When you send out good vibes, you attract good vibes back, in the form of inspiration, events, "lucky" breaks, conditions, circumstances, helpful people, etc., which contribute to achieving and receiving your desires. In essence, this is the Law of Attraction at work. As doors are opened, opportunities arise, and you feel inspired to take action to better your life.

Consider life to be like a spiral of good and bad experiences. Generally you are never static, as you are either moving up or down the spiral. What you often do not realize is that the choice of direction is yours.

The impact of your thoughts and feelings is momentous. One seemingly insignificant thought builds on another. If you ignore the negative feelings that indicate your low vibes (even if you are grumbling over something like the weather or the person who took your parking space), it may not seem as though these feelings are making a big difference. However, each negative thought engenders a negative feeling and attracts more bad experiences to you rather than good ones.

To understand the ramifications of your thoughts and feelings, consider navigation at sea. If you are off course by one degree, then you would be heading miles off target, and that makes all the difference as to whether or not you reach your desired destination.

Just as the Law of Gravity has been proven through life experiences (drop an apple and it will fall to the ground) so has the Law of Attraction been proven through life experiences (good vibes attract good experiences, bad vibes attract bad experiences). The difference is that the Law of Gravity was explained by science many centuries ago, and it is only now that quantum physics is beginning to explain the Law of Attraction.

Chapter Summary

- Through exploring the following two aspects of ancient wisdom that are proven by modern science a crucial link emerges...

1. Energy Alignment - At the core of all holistic therapies. It involves many different techniques to enhance your general energy levels. As your energy levels improve, your energy begins to flow more freely and fully within your body and you feel better.

2. Law of Attraction - The better you feel, the higher levels of health you enjoy and the better and happier the life experiences you attract. There will be better career and earning opportunities, loving relationships and an all-round happier life because the better you feel, the more inspired you feel, the more you are attracted to events, people and circumstances that help you fulfill your desires.

Energy Alignment:
The better your energy levels = The better you feel

The Law of Attraction:
The better you feel = The happier and more fulfilling
life experiences you attract

- Your feelings are a clear indication of your energy levels; whether your energy is in alignment and whether you are fully benefiting from the Law of Attraction.

Chapter 3

Energy Levels

In the last Chapter we explored how our thoughts change the frequency of our energy waves, which in turn change our feelings. We also noted that the functioning of the chakras is affected by how we think. So, when we think about things that make us feel bad, the chakras start to close, our energy flow is reduced and our energy levels drop. Conversely when we think about things that make us feel good, the chakras begin to open again, our energy flows more fully and our energy levels increase. We will now take a practical perspective of how this impacts the experiences we attract into our lives.

If you are familiar with the Law of Attraction but still have some desires that have been eluding you, the missing piece to the puzzle is energy flow.

Energy Flow

Holistic therapies take different approaches but aim to achieve the same result: optimizing the energy flow of the body. In essence, this balances the chakras so that they function properly.

Yoga postures activate and balance the chakras. Sound therapy is simple, yet effective, and has been used for centuries because it affects the mindset and mood, and therefore the chakras of the listener. Aromatherapy works on the vibration of smell and herbal medicine uses the vibration of energy in foods. Colour therapy also works on the principle of improving the vibrational energies to coax the chakras back into balance so they resonate fully again.

Your energy levels impact your quality of thinking, your decision-making, your power to influence, your ability to pick up on opportunities and inspirational ideas. Your energy levels also heavily impact your ability to effectively execute what needs to be done in order to achieve your desires.

The Body's Energy Field

Quantum physics has documented that all material substances, such as trees, rocks, animals and humans, have subtle interdependent energy fields because they are all composed of similar particles.

Centuries ago, the term *aura* was given to the energy field surrounding each person. It is created by the vibration from the energy flowing through the chakras and consists of seven layers of increasingly fine vibrating energy particles. A section of the aura is often depicted on spiritual paintings as a halo over the crown of the head. For those people who are trained, or who can instinctively see the complete aura of a healthy body, it looks like the hazy glow of a rainbow. Everyone has the ability to sense auras and does so when picking up on good or bad vibes from another person.

Thoughts and Feelings Affect Energy

When an event in your life results in you becoming emotionally shut down, the chakras also shut down. The emotional blocks cause energetic blocks, which lead to physical blocks, and the result over time is ill health.

When you speak of feeling "open," what you are saying is literally true: the chakras are open and the energy flows more fully, with the result that you look radiant.

There are many common expressions that reflect the impact that the vibrations from your thoughts have on your energy. The more positive the thought and emotion you experience, such as love, the higher the frequency, and the more likely you are to feel "uplifted," "over the moon" and "on a high" with increased energy levels.

Remember the last time you were with someone who is highly charged, someone who is a real live-wire, who is stimulating, uplifting, light-hearted, on your own wavelength and on a frequency that you resonate and feel in tune with? This person does you a power of good. You may be buzzing and

14

feel lighter, feel energized, re-charged and invigorated, empowered, energetic, refreshed, rejuvenated, revived and enlightened as a result. Clearly the good feelings experienced are reflected in the higher energy levels enjoyed.

By contrast, have you ever experienced these feelings: Emotionally knocked flat, down-trodden, hitting rock bottom, going on the downward spiral, having that sinking feeling, like your life is spinning out of control, feeling downbeat, worn out, washed-out, burnt-out, rundown, sluggish, stuck in a rut, run into the ground, running on empty, or feeling low, heavy, stagnant and lifeless?

If something happens that you do not feel good about, it may make you go downhill quickly and so may make you feel exhausted, drained, depleted, shattered, out of kilter, depressed and sapped of energy.

The words commonly used to describe the thoughts that give you low moods are also describing the low state of energy within the body as a result of the effect that these thoughts have on the chakras.

The more negative and emotionally shut down you feel, the more your chakras are also likely to be shut down and out of balance. Conversely, the more positive your thoughts and feelings are, the more energetic you feel and the more open, balanced and in alignment your chakras are.

So you open and close your chakra valves by how you think and therefore feel, and if one of the chakras is shut down and out of balance it will have an effect on the other chakras and on their associated bodily systems. Your energy system is so finely tuned that even a small mood swing shows the change in the energy balance of the body. This impacts your health and your actions, potentially setting limits on what you accomplish. How you think and feel therefore affects your energy levels, your life experiences and so your reality.

Thoughts Producing Good Feelings Help Balance Energy

Thoughts that make you feel genuinely happy are obviously good for you. When you feel happy, you feel less stress. Every time something affects your mind, it also affects your body. If something wonderful happens and you feel full of joy, then endorphins, mood-enhancers that reduce stress levels, will be pumped around your body.

The British Heart Foundation, seeking to raise awareness of ways to prevent heart disease, organized a laugh-a-thon because having a good laugh has such a beneficial effect and helps prevent heart disease. The physiological effects of laughter on the body are significant because they change hormone levels in the bloodstream. Laughter also regulates blood pressure, and gives an all-around boost to the immune system. It increases the vascular blood flow, which helps increase the oxygenated flow of blood through the body to feed, nourish and heal the body's cells and internal organs.[4]

Scientists confirm that laughter actively stimulates important healing chemicals in the immune system with the production of lymphocytes containing T-cells, the Natural Killer immune cells and interferon-gamma that are vital to keeping the body healthy.[5]

When you genuinely feel good, you are much more likely to have a better night's sleep and so your body has a greater chance of recuperating. Not only does the high you have from feeling good and having fun recharge your body, it also keeps your mind more alert, improves concentration, relieves mental stress, helps you make better decisions and allows you to be more receptive to ideas and opportunities.

Think of the last time you had a really good belly laugh and remember how you felt afterwards. It feels great; it gives you a natural high that can lift you out of the lowest of moods.

Toddlers laugh 300-400 times a day, whereas adults only laugh around 15 times a day, if that. In this culture, high stress levels are accepted as the norm and people feel guilty if they are seen relaxing and having fun rather than working hard. Many subconsciously consider that being stressed in their jobs equates to how important they are at work. Those who work at home looking after families often put themselves at the bottom of the pile; looking after everyone else first. Tiredness, exhaustion, resentment, anger, dissatisfaction,

---

4   *Humour Improves Health*, Brain Waves, Society for Neuroscience (Summer 2002)
5   Science Correspondent, *The Times* (2.9.2003), Science Editor, *The Telegraph* (22.7.2003)

frustration, shutting down, having arguments, and feeling no joy can all easily be the end result.

Scientists have documented significant biological changes that happen in the body when we move down through the emotions from happy to sad.

Many of us overlook what is happening to our bodies when we feel anxious, sad or stressed. When the stress hormone adrenalin is pumped around the body, the immune system is compromised. The blood vessels constrict and this raises blood pressure and increases the number of platelets that can cause obstructions in arteries, thereby causing potential heart problems. The flow of blood to the skin, vital organs and digestive systems is also slowed down and diverted to the muscles ready for "fight or flight," causing the organs to receive lower amounts of the nourishment needed for health and vitality.

By tuning into the higher vibrations that the body naturally resonates with when you feel good, you are literally rising above and emitting stronger, healthier, happier vibes around yourself so that your health and life can regain balance.

Spending your time anxiously focusing on an illness or condition generates additional stress hormones and only serves to aggravate problems. If you are ill but make a commitment to yourself to take your mind off your symptoms by finding things to focus your attention on that will make you feel good, even laugh (such as funny films, being with great friends, etc.), your immune system will be boosted, the cells of your body will start to relax and so begin to heal themselves naturally. When you are in so much pain, or you are really worried about your health problems, this may seem a frivolous idea to try…but it does work.

The body rebuilds itself every day. Broken bones, cuts and bruises all heal, many cells die and are replaced with new ones. Your skeleton is totally renewed every three months. Every 72 hours the entire lining of your stomach is replaced and your skin is renewed every 5 weeks. Even if 75 percent of someone's liver is removed by surgery, it can regain its original mass in two to three weeks.

The body naturally heals itself except when there is an interruption of energy flow due to the physical side effects of stress coming from negative feelings.

Renowned physician and author, Bernie Siegel, M.D., wrote a series of books that include true stories of many so called "terminally ill" patients who achieved remissions and cures. His observations led him to understand the significant importance of the physiological effect of emotions.[6]

Most actions that are basic to our survival instinctively feel good to us. When stressed, some of the body's available water supply is needed for the breakdown of stored materials like proteins, starch and fat. The latest scientific research has documented that water is extremely effective in helping to bring back health to a stressed body.

We can survive without food for a few weeks but we can only survive without water for a few days, since the human body is comprised of over 80% water. Water transports elements such as hormones and nutrients; it removes waste products and has an essential role in all aspects of the body's metabolic functions, including water-dependent chemical reactions. Hydration is vital to human health and this is why it feels so good to drink water when thirsty.

Although it feels good to eat food when hungry, it is still worth observing how various different foods affect you. Some foods will make you feel energized, while others will leave your body feeling drained and sluggish. These feelings show the state of your chakras.

The reason that you are likely to find tasting delicious food, singing, dancing, breathing deeply, belly laughing, admiring fabulous artwork, sitting in a beautifully decorated room or wearing your favourite clothes so empowering and energizing is because they are all stimulating your senses. This makes you think good thoughts, feel good feelings, help your chakras to regain balance and optimize your energy levels.

---

6   Bernie Siegel, M.D., *Peace, Love, Healing* (Quill, 1998).

18

Feelings Give Guidance

Worries are the cause of sleepless nights, aging, tension and stress. Negative thoughts, which produce negative emotions, literally drain away your time and energy. These thoughts lower your vibrations, restricting and closing down the chakras. The chakras are unable to resonate fully and cannot draw as much energy into your body. When this happens, your life does not flow as well as it could.

The poisonous thoughts literally poison and sicken the body. When you change your focus from something that makes you feel bad to something that makes you feel genuinely more positive, you are changing the frequency of your feelings.

Consider a standard light switch that can be flicked on or off. Now consider a dimmer switch, which is used to restrict the supply of electricity so that the light is only partially on. Even though the full electrical energy is still available, the dimmer switch acts as a resistance to allow only a portion of the electrical supply to flow.

When there is resistance in an electric circuit, the amount of energy available to the bulb is reduced so the light is dimmed. When you have negative thoughts, you may not be aware of what you are doing, but your thoughts are creating resistance in the body. As the body needs a certain amount of energy to function at optimum health, the greater your resistance or negativity, the lower the flow of energy, the lower the level of health enjoyed and the more despondent you feel.

If, rather than having negative thoughts and feelings, you took a different point of view so that you did not let issues affect you so much, the energy or electrochemical impulses from the brain would be allowed to flow with greater freedom. This releases the resistance (the negative thought patterns), which means that an increased electrical current is allowed to flow so you feel much brighter and greater health is enjoyed.

If you ignore the fact that your thoughts are negative and continue to feel low, it won't make a difference in the short term, just as ignoring a low charge on a battery won't have much of an impact short term. However, if you continue to ignore it, there will come a time when the charge on your battery is so depleted that the energy is likely to drain out and become flat.

The same applies when you ignore the negative thoughts that produce your negative feelings. Your energy becomes drained and your ability to heal is depleted, leading to ill health and the continued attraction of negative experiences. By retraining your negative thought patterns, (which set up your beliefs) toward the positive, you will feel much better and become more vibrant.

The Power Of Belief

Beliefs can be shaped by hearing a certain message repeated over and over again, by watching someone act a certain way repeatedly or by experiencing one quick dramatic event.

The story of drug trials during which a control group of individuals was given sugar pills offers a good illustration of the power of belief. Thinking they were being given the new Super Drug, those taking sugar pills regained their health and well-being because they believed they would. This placebo effect is well documented. The sugar pills were effective because of the belief placed in them by the individuals taking them.

A deeply instilled negative belief is equally powerful. Fear, disappointment, lack of self-worth, distrust of love and negative self-talk can all be the result of repeatedly hearing unintentionally harmful and belittling comments as a child while growing up.

The actions or beliefs of parents or someone of influence make a huge impression on children. The feelings portrayed can create vibes that children are very sensitive to and easily pick up on. The adult's words, actions, or lack of actions (such as lack of love) can result in the child holding limiting beliefs. These can become so ingrained in the subconscious mind of the child that they are still likely to be of influence when the child is an adult.

20

Do any of these phrases sound familiar to you?

You clumsy clot! ... You get what you deserve... Hi, Chubby... Don't be so stupid... You're such a scatterbrain... You're always in the way... You silly thing... Be quiet... Why do you talk so much? Shut up! ... Get out of my sight! Go away... Can't you do anything right? ... You're always late... Struggle is noble... You'll never amount to anything... You always look a mess... That's not good enough... Don't be so ambitious! ... Will you ever learn? ... Do you have to get everything wrong? ... Why do you always let me down? ... You're always unlucky in love... Money spoils you... Don't trust anyone or you'll get hurt... The poor get poorer... Success comes at a high price... You can't have money and free time... If you're successful, people will hate you, so it's best to just fit in... Nothing comes easy... Love leads to hurt... Money corrupts... No pain, no gain! ... Expect the worst and then anything else is a bonus... Don't get your hopes up...

Are the thoughts that create your own beliefs empowering you or holding you back?

You do not achieve what you are capable of but what you believe you are capable of. If you believe you can, you can. If you believe you can't, you can't...and won't.

Hidden Beliefs

Some of the peptides, which are the brain's chemical impulses created by emotions, are stored within the peptide receptors that are located in the organs and tissues around the body.[7] This may explain why there are so many reported cases of transplant patients who seem to acquire memories from their donors. For example, some acquire the taste for specific foods after the operation that are later found to be the favourites of the organ donor. This is a good example of how beliefs and memories can be buried deep within us, even if we are not consciously aware of them.

---

7   Dr. Candace Pert, *Molecules of Emotion: Why You Feel The Way You Feel* (Simon & Shuster, 1997).

Hidden Beliefs Can Sabotage Our Desires

Most people accept that a group of ten people can hold different beliefs over the same subject. Let us take love as an example. The adult who as a child had a traumatic event that left her feeling abandoned may not be consciously aware of any negative beliefs surrounding love. Yet, deep down she may have a hidden belief that links loving and trusting someone with the pain of being vulnerable to being abandoned again. This adult may therefore take a long time before feeling safe enough to have a close relationship.

This explains why the same events as adults affect us all differently and what one person finds ludicrous or irrelevant, another may find disturbing or devastating. When the hot button triggering your hidden belief is pushed, it may have a serious effect and impact your well-being and behavior.

If you notice a physical pain or an emotional overreaction whenever you experience certain events in your life, then it is quite likely that you have a hidden belief that is locked into your subconscious mind that is triggered whenever you find yourself in that particular situation. When the hidden limiting belief, caused by negative thoughts, sets off the emotional response, it also closes your chakras and affects your energy levels so you may feel off-colour, or unwell.

If you say you want an immensely successful business but have a strong hidden belief such as "You can't have money and free time as well..." then you may believe that you will have to work so hard that your family will resent your time away from them... and this may sabotage your chances of success.

Let us take another example, if your hidden belief is that you will never be rich, or that you are not good enough, you are unlikely to put yourself forward for promotion and may therefore stay at a lower salary.

Releasing Hidden Beliefs

You would not choose to hold onto limiting beliefs that are hidden in your subconscious mind if you were aware they were there and since you are the only person that can create your beliefs, you are also the only one who can change them.

When you understand energy alignment you can identify and release any limiting beliefs that cause the emotional blocks stopping you from achieving your desires. Surfing Rainbows is an effective technique to help you with this.

Although many of us are brought up to think that showing our emotions is a sign of weakness, at the core of each and every one of us is our emotion. That is what makes us who we are. Some may think that expressing emotions indicates a potential loss of control, which creates a sense of powerlessness. In reality, it is actually the holding onto negative emotions and negative thought patterns and beliefs that takes away control, because it draws in more negative situations, situations that no one would choose intentionally.

Extensive research shows that suppressing emotion does not eliminate the thoughts and feelings attached to them.[8] Instead, it actually attracts more of the same. Daniel Wegner, PhD, a professor of psychology at Harvard, called this the "rebound effect of thought suppression." Basically, it means that when you try to push away a thought you end up thinking about it more, as if each thought is a reliving of the event you seek to suppress. This sets up a vicious circle.

Self-Healing Our Bodies & Our Lives

Western medicine and holistic therapies all contribute greatly to improving health in their own ways. The premise of holistic therapies is that when the body is in balance (which is what happens when all your chakra valves are balanced and functioning fully) the body has sufficient energy flow to heal itself completely from physical ailments. This is quite a foreign concept to most of us who live in the West, but these therapies deliver results and are becoming more accepted and sought after.

---

8   Abramowitz JS, Tolin DF, Street GP, "Paradoxical Effects of Thought Suppression: A Meta-Analysis of Controlled Studies," *Clinical Psychology Review*. (2001): 683-703.
Gross JJ, Levenson RW, "Emotional Suppression: Physiology, Self Report, and Expressive Behavior." *Journal of Personality and Social Psychology*. (1993): 970-986
Roemer L, Borkovec TD. "Effects of Suppressing Thoughts About Emotional Material." *Journal of Abnormal Psychology*. (1994): 467,474.

Through understanding how your thoughts and feelings open or close your chakra valves and how this increases or reduces the energy flow to the different parts of the body, you can trace the symptoms within your body back to the emotional states that may have caused them. This has far-reaching implications for self-healing.

For complete healing to occur, you need to address what caused the problem or disease (dis-ease) in the first place, otherwise the symptoms simply recur.

A quick recap: thoughts produce chemical impulses called peptides and the largest groups of peptide receptors (which are the brain's system of communicating with the body in an effort to maintain good health) are concentrated in the locations up and down the spine that correspond to the chakras.[9] Each major chakra is also linked to particular parts of the body through its association with a nerve plexus, endocrine gland, lymphatic system and various organs. For example, the third chakra is associated with the solar plexus, the pancreas and adrenal glands, the digestive system and sympathetic nervous system and affects the organs in that area including the liver, stomach, gallbladder, spleen, and so on.

The chemical hormones secreted by the various endocrine glands have a dramatic effect, as do the nerve transmissions within the brain, spinal cord and peripheral nerves. For a very basic overview of the generally accepted associations of the chakras with the different parts of the body, please see Table 2 on page 176 titled "Self-Healing Your Body & Your Life."

When you understand the consequences of having thoughts, words and actions that result in negative feelings and low energy levels, and you consciously decide to change your perspective to take a genuinely more positive point of view, you are taking conscious control of your own health, happiness and life.

---

9   Dr. Candace Pert, *Molecules of Emotion: Why You Feel The Way You Feel* (Simon & Shuster, 1997).

Chapter Summary

- Your thoughts create your feelings and beliefs, and affect your energy levels (energy flow through your chakra energy centres).
- Your thoughts can either be empowering or limiting you. When an event in your life results in you becoming emotionally shut down, the chakra energy centres also shut down. The emotional blocks cause energetic blocks, which lead to physical blocks, and the result over time is ill health.
- Consider life to be like a spiral of good and bad experiences. Generally you are never static, as you are either moving up or down the spiral.
- When you speak of feeling "open," what you are saying is literally true: the chakra energy centres are open because you are thinking thoughts that make you feel good and the energy flows more fully, with the result that you are healthy, vibrant, feel refreshed and recharged.
- Surfing Rainbows offers simple steps to optimize your energy to achieve your desires and keep you on the upward spiral of good experiences in life.

Chapter 4

Balancing Energy Levels

In the last Chapter we explored how negative thoughts can create limiting beliefs, negative feelings and emotional blocks that lower energy levels.

The functioning of each energy centre chakra is affected by specific types of thoughts generating specific feelings. When we feel good in all these areas we are balancing our energy levels and releasing emotional blocks, thereby making it easier to achieve our dreams and desires.

Knowledge and understanding of the chakras was passed down from generation to generation by the ancient civilizations through word of mouth and by drawing symbols. Each chakra symbol, representing an energy centre, is based on a lotus flower and contains one or more Sanskrit vowels.

Chakra One
Trust

Chakra Two
Joy

Chakra Three
Self-Worth

Chakra Four
Love

Chakra Five
Positive
Self-Expression

Chakra Six
Inspiration

Chakra Seven
Enlightenment

Chakra One

Trust

How many times have you been told, "Just let go and trust; it will all turn out fine." Did it leave you wondering... *HOW?!*

When the first chakra is in balance, you feel safe and enjoy living with trust rather than living in fear. Located at the base of the spine, this chakra connects you to the physical world and keeps you grounded.

Those who do not trust often feel insecure and live in fear of failure, fear of change, or in fear of something (or someone) else. They either consciously or subconsciously rely on the opinions of others to gauge how they think they should feel, to make their decisions, and to determine their actions and reactions for them, succumbing to the whims of advertising and social pressures.

Trying to conform to what others think you should have or do can tie you up in knots. However, when you trust your feelings, you are tapping into a great source of inner wisdom that always provides you with accurate guidance in every situation. The more you trust and act on your feelings, the more receptive you become to receiving guidance in all areas of your life. Many people have evidence for themselves, or know of someone else, whose intuition has pulled them away from extreme danger by guiding them to take certain actions that just "felt right." There is also a wealth of subtle guidance available to us throughout our day for more commonplace situations.

How intensely we feel good or bad, happy or sad is a precise navigational system. This may sound very simplistic, but many of us rely much more heavily on what we think, or on what others say, rather than on what we feel is best.

The reason why it makes so much sense to trust your feelings is because they indicate whether you are thinking thoughts that are opening or closing your chakras, and so whether you are allowing greater or less energy to flow within your body...and therefore whether you are, or you are not, fully benefiting from the Law of Attraction.

Trusting your feelings simply means identifying how good or bad you feel about any topic; the more positive the response, the better the choice.

Whenever you have a decision to make, however tricky you think the decision is, try asking yourself, "Which option feels better?" Your answer about one option may come back to you as a physical sensation or an emotion you can identify, such as feeling relieved or sick to your stomach. If you have a few options to take but none of them feel good, stop and take a moment, delay taking any action and just ask yourself the same question again later. Relax and think about something else for a while.

As your mind rests, the answer will eventually come to you and it will just feel right. Even if you think you are procrastinating doing something, if it doesn't feel right to do it, it isn't a good choice for you at that time. If it feels bad, it is bad. If it feels good, it is good. When you are following this guidance you are always making the right decisions, and rather than forcing a solution that is likely to be the wrong one, you are being led to a solution as it evolves naturally.

This is very empowering. The safer you feel when trusting your feelings, the less you need to rely on other people's opinions and the less you need other crutches like addictions.

When you do not trust your feelings to guide you but instead have your mind so fixed on how you should solve a problem, you can be closed to more appropriate options that are presented to you. For example, you may feel the need to be in a relationship with one particular person to be happy, but there may be potentially better matches. Or, you may have your mind fixed on earning money from one particular source when there may be a multitude of different options available.

Another example of not trusting the inner guidance of your feelings comes when you allow yourself to be caught up in the advice or opinions of others, even when it does not feel right for you. Sometimes it is difficult to look past the advice of experts, family and influential friends when their views imply that you cannot have your desires. However, when you believe their negative opinions, you allow their point of view to limit your outlook and it blocks you from achieving your goals. You need to find the strength and determination to believe in the guidance that comes from within, as it can lead you around any obstacle to find the solution to enjoy *any* desire.

An expert opinion is very persuasive, and if you were alive when the comments below were made, you may well have trusted their words, but it is clear that the opinions were wrong.

- Western Union's opinion of Alexander Graham Bell's Telephone in 1876 was that "the device is inherently of no value to us."
- Sir Preece, Chief Engineer of Britain's General Post Office, in 1876 said "We do not have need of a telephone; we have plenty of messenger boys."
- The President of the Royal Society in 1895 said that "Heavier than air flying machines are impossible."
- The Commissioner of patents in 1899 said that "everything that can be invented, has been invented."
- The Harvard Economic Society published the opinion that "a severe depression like that of 1920-21 is outside the range of probability" in their Weekly Letter 16 Nov 1929.

- Thomas Watson Jr, Head of IBM in 1943 said, "I think there is a world market for maybe five computers."

Let these notes serve as a helpful reminder that the so-called "experts" are not always right. There is no need to trust what others say. Asking for an opinion is fine but what you choose to do with it is your decision. Life becomes so much easier when you understand that, rather than putting your trust in anyone or anything else, you just need to trust your own feelings: trust how you feel about what others say.

The more you learn to trust your feelings to guide you, the more you release your fears.

The emotional state that affects this first chakra impacts all the others. Trusting your own feelings is crucial. When you allow your feelings to guide your thoughts, it is likely that you feel secure and your first chakra will be functioning properly. Being able to trust yourself grounds you and that makes you feel secure in your world.

The more you trust the guidance that comes from your feelings, the more evidence you will receive that it is accurate, and the more you will feel safe, calm and secure during your day, every day.

Summary

When Chakra One is in balance you feel safe and secure; living with trust rather than living in fear. (This impacts your ability to make good decisions and take advantage of ideas and opportunities that come your way.)

Tip: Trusting your feelings simply means identifying how good or bad you feel about any topic and then using that guidance to determine your next thoughts, words and actions.

Quick Check

To find out if Chakra One is balanced, answer this question: How good does this statement feel to you on a scale of 0-10?

I feel safe trusting my feelings to guide my thoughts, words and actions so that I always make the best choices throughout my day, and am guided to achieving my desires.

(If you find it easier, you can just give an instinctive response on how you are feeling e.g., very bad, bad, good, very good, every time that the scale of 0-10 is referred to in this book.)

Chakra Two

Joy

You may have been told to be happy and stay happy even when you do not have something that you have really wanted for a long time, but you may wonder …HOW ?!

When you feel really happy, the second chakra is likely to be functioning fully. This chakra relates to enjoying the various pleasures in life; living a life of joy and appreciation rather than one of sadness and disappointment. It is located in the pelvis and is associated with creativity.

Since life comprises a stream of unfolding desires during the time between thinking about a new desire and actually enjoying it, it is important to try to stay focused on the joy of why you want what you want, rather than on the worries and upset about not having it yet.

Whenever you feel frustrated, desperate or negative in any way, it is good to acknowledge how you feel. All negative feelings are there for a reason, they are there to guide you. When you ignore how you feel, it only makes the situation worse, because if you are unhappy, you are attracting more unhappiness.

When in a situation that causes great unhappiness or anxiety, it helps to ask if there is another point of view that could be taken. By looking for ways to feel better and more hopeful, eventually you will feel genuinely more positive about the issue. By intentionally adjusting your perspective to take conscious control over your thoughts, you can limit the negative impact of a painful situation.

When you have wanted something for a long time, you may not feel very hopeful or happy about the prospect of ever enjoying it, but that is causing the problem because it is the high vibes you have when you feel good that are needed to attract your desires.

How long should you keep aiming to feel good about achieving your desire? The simple answer has to be, until you achieve it, if that is what you want. This is because when you start a quest to reach something, but stop in your tracks halfway, it is unlikely that you will ever arrive.

Abraham Lincoln failed in business twice, was defeated for the Legislature, for Speaker, for Congress, for Senate, and he was also defeated for Vice President before he was elected President in 1860. He wanted to become the President of the United States … and he did.

Some of us have been conditioned from childhood to "not raise our hopes too high" when we want something, in case we are disappointed. This limiting attitude is the surest way to be disappointed. When you raise your hopes and you are excited, you receive inspiring thoughts that help you gravitate towards what you want.

We are brought up in a society that tends to dwell on the negative, and so making a habit of finding things to focus our attention on that make us feel genuinely good may seem very foreign to many of us. You can go through life feeling down, sad and upset that your desires are unfulfilled, but this just repels your desires and pushes them further away from you. Instead, you can

34

go through life looking for ways to feel *genuinely* happier and hopeful. When you experience joy and consistently hold an optimistic perspective on any new desire that you would like to experience, your second chakra is likely to be functioning fully.

Summary

When Chakra Two is in balance you are living a life of joy and appreciation rather than one full of worries and disappointment.

Tip: By constantly focusing your attention on what makes you feel good… you will feel good. A simple way of maintaining high vibes throughout your day is to keep asking yourself … "What is the best thing about…" anything that happens in your day / your life / the people you meet etc.

Quick Check

To find out if Chakra Two is in balance, answer this question: How good do you feel, on a scale of 0-10, about your desires and your life in general?

If you feel bad in any way, then you are focusing on <u>not</u> having your desires and the result is that you feel disappointed, annoyed, jealous, etc. This attitude is repelling your desires. However, if you feel good when you answer the question it means you are attracting them faster.

Chakra Three

Self-Worth

You may want to improve your own self-confidence, but you may wonder ... HOW?!

When the third chakra is in balance, you have high self-worth. Located under the diaphragm, this chakra relates to our perception of ourselves and our response to outside stimulus.

When you judge your self-worth by how you think others judge you, you are giving your power away to those other people. And when you have low self-worth or low self-esteem, you are repelling your desires, because you do not feel good enough, or do not feel you deserve to have them. You don't feel able to accept what you want and so subconsciously push it away.

When you feel undeserving, you can quickly spiral down a vicious cycle, because as you repel your desires and believe you are not good enough, you attract more situations and more people that make you feel bad about yourself.

Children come into the world acting on their instincts. By the time a child reaches the age of seven their friends play a big part in how they feel about themselves. The group dynamic means that no one wants to stand out. They are now affected by the "attitude of the herd," explains Dr Christopher Green in *Beyond Toddlerdom*[10]. Children want to be just like their friends and to have the same things; they want to fit in and to be accepted.

The desire to please others, especially those we love, is a behavior we learn in childhood. When we are born we feel good about ourselves; we have no reason to think otherwise. As we grow up, our minds can become trapped in an uninspired, unempowered place that cannot attract the things we want.

Being able to define what we really want becomes masked by doing what is expected of us or what pleases others to gain their approval. Expectations and emotional beliefs are formed according to how other people think rather than by how we feel. This is at the core of why many of us grow up with a lack of self-confidence. Without trust in ourselves we can lose our confidence. When we lack confidence in ourselves, dreams can't be turned into reality, they just stay dreams. We then accept the notion that it is fine to settle for an unfulfilling life of compromise.

Children who are encouraged to rely on their own feelings will not doubt themselves quite so much as they grow up and will therefore be more likely to reach and achieve what they want in life as an adult.

Your level of self-worth comes from how you see yourself, and how you see yourself is up to you. It takes courage to take your power back. It is only your own approval that you need. Basing how you feel about yourself on other people's wishes is an impossible task as different people want different things, and it would be impossible to please them all.

---

10 Dr Christopher Green, *Beyond Toddlerdom,* Ebury Press (United Kingdom) 2007.

You deserve to believe that you are fabulous in your own wonderful way. After all, there has never been anyone just like you!

Surfing Rainbows will give you some tools to help improve your self-esteem and self-confidence so that you will be sending out stronger and stronger vibes and so attracting back more of what you want. This in itself will give you more self-confidence.

When you feel good as a result of having high self-worth, your third chakra is more likely to be functioning fully, and, rather than blocking, you are allowing your desires to come into your life.

Summary

When Chakra Three is in balance you feel deserving and have a good perception of yourself (allowing you to accept your desires).

Tip: Take your time over the self-esteem improving exercises that you will be introduced to when you start Surfing Rainbows.

Quick Check

To find out if Chakra Three is in balance, answer this question: How good do you feel on, a scale of 0-10, about yourself?

(When you feel good, you expect, attract and welcome your desires. When you feel bad about yourself, you push yourself away from them.)

Chakra Four

Love

You may have been told to relax, open up and let others into your heart. That is easier than it sounds for many people, and they may wonder... *HOW?!*

The fourth chakra is located in the heart area and when it is in balance you are living with love; loving others, loving yourself and loving your life.

You may go through life being shy and guarded, trying to protect your heart. This limits your ability to attract loving relationships. When your heart is fully open, you can enjoy loving relationships while feeling reassured that you are being totally protected through your inner guidance.

To be able to accept love, you need to be able to accept that you are lovable. To accept yourself as lovable you need to appreciate your uniqueness. The tenderness and care you would want to give to someone else are the same emotions you need to have for yourself. Clearly, the more loving you are to yourself and to others in general, the more you are likely to attract love back.

Let us look at what happens in an example where your immediate response to a friend's actions is that you feel angry. If you think about things that make you angry, you will feel angrier. If you immediately vent your anger with that person, this negative approach can quickly spiral downwards and may negatively affect the rest of your life, like a falling set of dominos.

So, in this example, if you choose to think first before you respond, you can change your outlook and therefore how you feel which paves the way for calmer dialogue. Remember that we get back what we send out. Every action starts with a thought, so aim to take conscious control of the direction in which your thoughts are heading.

All that you need to know about any relationship is revealed to you by how good it feels to you. If you want to check how good a match someone is to you on a personal or professional basis, ask yourself how good you feel about the person in general on a scale of 0-10. If it feels good, then it is good.

When you appreciate certain aspects of a person, but do not feel comfortable with other aspects, you may make the decision that it is no longer right for this person to be as close a friend as they have been. However, as you keep focusing on what makes you feel genuinely good about everyone you know and everyone you come into contact with, you will be attracting more of the qualities you like in the people you are already with, and in the new people you meet. When you have high vibes, you are attracting relationships of the same quality.

When you feel good because you are open to loving yourself and others, your fourth chakra is more likely to be in balance.

Summary

When Chakra Four is in balance you are living with love (which results in being open to people presenting ideas and opportunities).

Tip: For instant, accurate feedback when you want to check how good a match someone is to you on a personal or professional basis, ask yourself how good you feel on a scale of 0-10 about the person in general.

Tip: By focusing on the positive qualities that you like most in everyone, you will soon be attracting more people that rate a 10 (or a 10+!) with those qualities who will enrich and support your life.

Quick Check

To find out if Chakra Four is in balance, answer this question: How good do you feel, on a scale of 0-10, whenever you think about all the people in your life?

Chakra Five

Positive Self-Expression

You may have been told to think positively, but you may be wondering ... *HOW?!* when so many worries keep coming to mind.

When your fifth chakra is in balance, you engage in sincere positive expression. Located in the base of the throat, this chakra closes down when we engage in negative expression and opens up when we feel genuinely good about whatever we are communicating through our thoughts, words and actions.

Criticizing, blaming, pre-judging or justifying yourself means focusing on negative thoughts and therefore results in sending out negative vibes, and this just attracts more negative experiences back.

Many people regard positive thinking as a way of ignoring or masking problems and pretending that everything is fine by hiding how they feel.

They may think that putting on a brave face is a positive response to what is happening. When asked, the tendency would be to say that all is well, when actually they feel pretty rotten.

You are not supposed to ignore what is happening around you right now, nor does it make sense to fake, deny, disregard or to be embarrassed by how you feel. Rather than lying to yourself or to anyone else, the way to keep your Chakra Five in balance is to be totally honest with yourself about how you feel. The outward mask is irrelevant here. What is crucial is to determine how you really feel. Then by acknowledging, accepting and releasing the negative, and consciously moving towards a genuinely more positive point of view about whatever you are thinking, saying and doing, you will improve how you feel about the situation.

You do have the choice about what you think, say and do. When you choose what to eat, you choose what you like. When you choose what music to listen to, you choose what you like and what makes you feel good. In the same way, when you think, say or do anything, you can consciously choose what makes you feel good and focus on how you *would like* the situation to unfold or to improve. It is this use of intention, the conscious guiding of your thoughts and feelings that maintains balanced energy levels. You naturally feel happier when you think about things that make you feel good. The happier you are, the more your energy is in alignment.

By allowing your feelings to guide you in choosing your best thoughts, words and actions, you are choosing to take the upward direction on the spiral of life.

If you are in the middle of a situation that you would like to see improved, take a moment to look at the event from a different point of view. Rather than dwell on things that are making you unhappy, find something that makes you feel more hopeful. When you have positive self-expression and stay optimistically focused on your desires, your fifth chakra stays in balance and helps you achieve them.

Summary

When Chakra Five is in balance you are genuinely feeling good about whatever you are communicating through your thoughts, words and actions.

Tip: Try to remember that you clearly feel happier when you think about things that make you feel good, and the happier you are, the more your energy is in alignment.

Quick Check

To find out if Chakra Five is in balance, answer this question: How good do you feel, on a scale of 0-10, about what you are saying, doing and thinking?

Chakra Six

Inspiration

Some people always seem to have inspirational ideas and their exciting lives seem to flow smoothly. Have you ever wondered *HOW* you could encourage inspiration to flow so that solutions to your own problems become clearer more quickly?

The sixth chakra, centered on the forehead, is also known as the third eye and it is concerned with inspiration, insight and clarity.

By allowing your mind to switch off for a while, you become more in tune with your feelings. Ideas and inspiration will come easily, turning your action into inspired action. Inspired action never feels bad, it never feels like hard work or drudge, it always feels right.

Some ways of relaxing may take more time out of your day than others and some may require a little forward planning, such as playing golf, having a facial, going swimming, going for a walk or having a relaxing bath. For some people, being still and doing nothing will be the answer, while for others their minds will only rest when they are being active and absorbed in something totally unrelated to their worries. Perhaps the answer for them will be painting, swimming, running or playing tennis.

We live in a culture where we think we cannot afford to take the time out to relax. Taking the time to allow the pace of life to stop for a moment allows your body to let go of the adrenalin rush that is a bodily response to stress. Even though the advantages of relaxing may be obvious, few people take the time to do it every day, maybe because they consider relaxation a luxury rather than a basic necessity.

Time is of the essence in today's fast-paced world. We are so busy, and our minds are so full, that we often miss valuable opportunities and insights. Inspired action may include having the hunch to make a quick phone call to an old friend, to go on a trip somewhere new, or to chat with a stranger. Whatever the hunch is, it often leads to results that you may still not have achieved after years and years of taking uninspired action.

Allowing your body to relax gives it a chance to regain balance and allow inspiration to flow.

Taking time out from your life to relax ensures clarity of thought, it helps you step back so that you can see issues more clearly and it helps you manage your time, yourself and others more effectively. Far from being time wasted, time spent relaxing saves you much more time in the long run. It helps you realize your desires much faster because during relaxation you are allowing your feelings to guide your thoughts. When you want to achieve a number of things in a short space of time, and you want to swiftly materialize your desires, inspired action assisted by relaxation allows unlimited access to your intuitive guidance. When you feel inspired, your sixth chakra is in balance and functioning fully.

Summary

When Chakra Six is in balance, inspiration, insight and clarity are the result, (helping fulfill goals faster).

Tip: Encourage inspiration to flow by asking yourself a question about anything that you want guidance on, but rather than letting your mind answer the question, just relax and see what springs to mind. The answer will either come quickly or eventually. Either way you will know if it is right by how good it feels to you.

Quick Check

To find out if Chakra Six is in balance, answer this question: How good do you feel, on a scale of 0-10? (When you feel good you feel relaxed and this allows inspiration to flow.)

For instant, accurate feedback about whether the action you are considering is inspired action, ask yourself how good you feel about it on a scale of 0-10.

Chakra Seven

Enlightenment

You may have heard the expression, "relax and enjoy the journey," but if you have worries on your mind, you may be left wondering… *HOW?!*

When your seventh chakra, the energy vortex of the highest vibration, is in balance, you feel able to live in the moment. Located at the top of the head and also known as the Crown Chakra, this chakra links you to the highest aspects of yourself. You feel a deep connection to oneness and universal energy and you feel at peace and contented.

Taking a look at the never-ending cycle of dreaming up and materializing new desires helps to explain the idea of enjoying the journey. Many people wrestle with the upset of not having achieved certain things in their lives, but they will never achieve everything they want because as one desire is fulfilled, so a new desire is born. That is how our lives evolve, and that is how we grow.

When you see or experience something that you do or do not like, it helps you decide what you would, or would not, like to experience from then on. Having decided that you want something new, if you then adopt the attitude that you cannot be happy until you have it, your energy will be out of balance, focusing on the unhappiness of *not having*. Your vibrational energy will be forever repelling this new desire for as long as you are feeling bad about it.

If you change your point of view and release the disappointment and struggle and then intentionally shift your outlook to one of being happy about the prospect of enjoying your desire, you take on a totally different outlook. With this different perspective you understand that the time between dreaming up your new desire and actually enjoying it in your reality is a useful time to become absolutely clear about the various qualities of what you want. This helps you to keep redefining your desire until you have it.

From this new standpoint, you will be feeling good within yourself, and so your energy will be in balance. As you keep focusing on things that feel good to you, your energy naturally radiates these good feelings and you are attracted to coincidences, chance meetings and drawn to take inspired action. If your attention is sidetracked, then something that may feel better to you will grab your attention. You will gravitate towards this new action and continue to have the impulse to follow new hunches so that you attract and fulfill your desires quickly.

The cycle then starts over again as you dream up another new desire, which you either feel good or bad about, and so you either materialize it quickly, slowly or not at all.

You can shift your energy from repelling to attracting what you want in your life by how you are feeling throughout your day. By being totally focused on what makes you feel good during every moment of your day, you cannot be worried about your future or upset about the past.

By allowing yourself to live in the present, enjoying your day, feeling good, feeling relaxed, you are keeping your chakras in balance and you are following your inner wisdom and moving towards your desires.

When you are feeling negative, you are going in the wrong direction, and moving away from your desires. Since you have control of your thoughts and your thoughts shape your beliefs and actions, focusing your attention on the things that please you instead of the things that displease you means that you also have control of how you feel, and that means you have control of which direction you are heading in. The choice is yours.

This is where it all comes full circle.

By mastering how to trust your feelings and allowing them to guide your thoughts, words and actions, you receive accurate guidance on where to focus your attention, and so you enjoy living with the positive attributes of having all your chakras in balance. You become more inspired and enlightened because you are living with trust, joy, high self-worth, love and positive expression. When you benefit from having these qualities in your life, you are aligned with your inner wisdom and you actively embrace the real meaning of love for yourself, for others and for life itself.

It is no wonder that you feel so good, so very good, and know confidently that you are going in the right direction to reach your desires…and this is of course what makes it easy to live in the present and enjoy every moment of your day. Relax and enjoy where you are on the journey, and the actual journey will take care of itself, because when you are enjoying yourself, you are following your inner guidance towards achieving each of your never-ending stream of unfolding desires.

When this happens you are Surfing Rainbows.

Summary
When Chakra Seven is in balance you feel at peace, contented and able to live in the moment.

Tip: By being totally focused on what makes you feel good during every moment of your day you cannot be worried about your future or upset about your past. It also means that you are allowing your feelings to guide you so that you really can relax and enjoy your day, your life, your journey.

Quick Check

To find out if Chakra Seven is in balance, answer this question: How good do you feel on a scale of 0-10?

(If you feel bad in any way, then you are not enjoying the moment to moment of your journey. If you feel good, then you are.)

Chapter Summary

- Energy alignment results in releasing the emotional blocks that would otherwise stop you from achieving your desires.
- Energy alignment happens when focusing on the thoughts and feelings that open the seven chakras.
- As your vibes become higher because your energy flows more freely, you attract your desires much faster because inspiration flows and you are attracted to events, people, information and circumstances that help you fulfill those desires.

www.SurfingRainbows.com/Surfing
offers more ideas, hints, suggestions and
exercises to help you keep your chakras
open, to raise your vibes and take full
advantage of the Law of Attraction.

Chapter 5

The Promise of Surfing Rainbows

The Promise of Surfing Rainbows supports, clarifies and goes beyond the emerging understanding of the importance of feelings. All the "quick checks" throughout the last Chapter have shown that the better you feel, the more your energy is in balance. Now take a look at the Table titled "The Surfing Rainbows Crucial Link" on page 172, and you will notice that the emotional states required for successfully achieving your desires are the same as when all your chakras are in balance.

As you allow your feelings to guide your thoughts through Surfing Rainbows, you can be absolutely sure that you are benefiting from the crucial link in ancient wisdom to optimize your energy flow and raise your vibes sufficiently to attract your desires.

Genuinely feeling good is key. We are born instinctively knowing how to do this, but as we grow up we seem to forget or have it "educated" out of us. Naturally it is much better never to forget rather than to have to remember it again later, and this was the reasoning behind writing *The Promise of Surfing Rainbows Storybook* for children (please turn to page 212 to see the synopsis).

It would be easy and correct to say that all you have to do is feel good. Indeed, the continuous process of releasing resistance, releasing resistant thoughts, to regain your energy balance is a natural process. However, when you are faced with a problem, or when you are upset about a desire that continues to elude you, feeling good to bring your energy back into balance can be tremendously tough.

When you feel lost, desperate, in a panic, or simply sidetracked by worries, that is when you can get stuck in a rut. Over time, this new not-so-good feeling becomes the norm, and your reality can become steadily worse.

Surfing Rainbows helps you ease the process of regaining your energy alignment. It is about having fun, feeling good and creating the life you love living.

Many of us are brought up to believe that for a concept to be of any value, it has to be difficult to understand. Surfing Rainbows is extremely simple and yet extremely effective. It costs nothing to try it, and if you do it properly, the results will speak for themselves.

You will be encouraged to change your outlook to a genuinely more positive point of view. You cannot feel bad when you feel good, and the better you feel, the more your chakras are in balance and the higher your energy levels become and that makes you feel better still.

The better you feel, the higher your energy levels, the better your vibes and the faster you are attracting your desires. This is what happens when you are Surfing Rainbows.

There is no need to take a massive leap of faith or to adopt an unquestioning attitude. Consider a few small desires and start Surfing Rainbows for them. As each desire is achieved, become more confident. Become more excited. Become more convinced! Then try Surfing Rainbows for a more important goal. See more results. Become more convinced. As you prove to yourself that Surfing Rainbows really does work, you will find it invaluable as part of your everyday life. When you are truly Surfing Rainbows, your infinite potential meets unlimited possibilities.

When we are Surfing Rainbows and life just seems to flow we have our energy in alignment which means we are not fearful, sad or disappointed. We also do not feel undeserving or bad about ourselves, and we do not feel alone or unloved. When we are truly Surfing Rainbows we are unconcerned about all the things that would otherwise have worried us. Living a life free of these constraining thoughts may seem unlikely to many people but as you begin Surfing Rainbows you will see that it really is possible.

In the Inspiring Notes Section on page 195 you will meet many people who have had tough problems to contend with, but they all managed to release the chains that were holding them back so that they could achieve their dreams.

Even though their dreams are unlikely to be the same as yours, the intention of including all the true stories in this book is not to imply that you should be aiming for similar desires but rather they are there to inspire you and to give you a gentle reminder that your dreams are achievable as well.

"Having spent until the age of thirty two working in the wrong jobs, married to the wrong partner, driving the wrong car and living the wrong life I can categorically tell you that the wonderful message from Surfing Rainbows that you can love your life and that you can live your dreams is not only inspirational, it is also deadly accurate. As a young, working class man I was told by my peers that 'people like us' do not become artists, they do not write books and they certainly do not have films made about their life.

I was also told that my very small reality was the only reality, and that I should be grateful for my meagre lot. Tired of living a lie and depressed by my life in the lower echelons of thought I decided to prove folklore wrong. Convinced that there must be more to life, I decided to become a martial arts instructor (and was later polled as the number one self defense instructor in the world by Black Belt magazine USA). I then followed this by living out another dream...the dream of becoming a writer.

I wrote my first book in a factory toilet where I was hired to sweep floors. My world was so small that I did not even know anyone that owned a typewriter, so the odds for my success were so minute that they did not even attract official odds. and yet that first book, Watch My Back still went onto become a Sunday Times Best Seller, a BAFTA winning short film (Brown Paper Bag), a £2million pound BIFFA nominated feature film (Clubbed) that premiered in London, Birmingham and Paris and (this year) an Oscar long-listed half hour film called Romans 12:20.

I am an ordinary person, let us have no doubt about that. So if I can attract an amazing life I know that anyone can do it. I wish I'd have known about Surfing Rainbows way back when I started; it would have saved me a lot of time. I love these beautifully presented books and I love this inspirational message and I highly recommend this work to anyone in the business of living a successful life."

Geoff Thompson

www.GeoffThompson.com

More detail is now given in relation to WHAT? WHEN? and WHY? you are encouraged to take the three steps to go Surfing Rainbows. The HOW to start Surfing Rainbows is found in Chapter 8.

There are three simple steps to Surfing Rainbows, and they are:

Step 1
Optimize Your Energy Levels in General
(The Feel-Good Lists, Energy Flow Chart & Improving
Your Self-Esteem Chart)

Step 2
Optimize Your Energy Levels in Relation to Your Desires
(Clarifying Desires, Stepping Stones, Releasing Resistance,
Creating Rainbow Expressions)

Step 3
Maintain Optimized Energy Levels
(The Golden Intention Code - Rainbow Viewing & Rainbow
Expressing)

Step 1

Surf Rainbows to Optimize Your Energy Levels in General

The Feel-Good Lists

Most of us have emotional triggers that help us forget about our worries for a while. You will be encouraged to make some Feel-Good Lists with ideas that will help you shift yourself into a better mood to give you that feel-good feeling.

You may think that the idea of making these lists is too trivial a task, but when your mood drops sharply you are naturally a lot less resourceful and so it is useful to prepare these lists in advance of when this happens, so that you can refer and use them as some quick pick-me-ups.

By intentionally focusing on things that make you feel good, you can acknowledge a situation that is troubling you without being controlled or overwhelmed by it.

Most of us would enjoy having more fun in our lives. When we take a moment to actually think about what would pepper our days with more fun, and then intentionally take the time to enjoy those things, we are enriching our lives.

Energy Flow Chart

The Energy Flow Chart is offered as a simple yet powerful tool to use whenever you face any problem. It helps you to clarify the issue, encourage a solution and uplift your mood.

By developing the habit of allowing your good and bad feelings to guide what you focus your attention on, you are helping yourself make subtle shifts in your energy levels throughout your day.

If you really do want to achieve what you say you want, then it is vital to keep shifting yourself into a more positive outlook. This is literally pivotal to Surfing Rainbows.

The Energy Flow Chart is particularly useful when you start Surfing Rainbows. This is because when you have been Surfing Rainbows for a little while, you will have many fulfilled desires to prove that it works, but at the beginning your mood may continue to dip because you may doubt that you can achieve the results you want. Past beliefs may mean that you keep going back to worries, or focusing on problems, or on situations that upset you. When this happens, the Energy Flow Chart can be used as a quick pocket-reminder to uplift you.

The better you feel, the faster you attract whatever you want. Do take note that the way to materializing *ALL* your desires is the same, however many desires you have, and that is by feeling better, because feeling better pulls your energy into alignment.

Improving Your Self-Esteem Chart

This is a chart with a few exercises that will start helping you improve your self-esteem. When you feel undeserving of your desires you often subconsciously block them from coming into your life. The exercises encourage you to embrace the uniqueness of who you are.

Step 2

Surf Rainbows to Optimize Your Energy Levels in Relation To Your Desires

Clarifying Your Desires

A few exercises will be offered that are aimed at clarifying your desires and encouraging new desires to evolve. It is so much easier to achieve something if you clearly know what you want.

Wanting is not just about material things. You may want to be happier, healthier, or more loved. The happier you are the more fun and relaxed you are to be around, and the more happiness you give others. When you have more, you have more to give.

When you want something but think it is not possible for you, it may be helpful to be reminded about some seemingly "impossible" desires that others have achieved. Here are some examples. Kevin Alderton, set the world outdoor blind ski record at 100.94 mph. Chris Klug won an Olympic medal after undergoing organ transplant surgery.

Don't allow your perception to create a barrier. Man, woman, boy or girl, nothing should ever stand between you and what you want to achieve. Age does not have to be a barrier to what you want either. Sally Cluley was 16 years old when she became a fully qualified pilot. Mark Zuckerberg, who is the creator of the website Facebook, is the youngest billionaire at the age of 23. And Soona Lee-Tolley managed a hole-in-one on the golf course at the age of 5.

The Kentucky Fried Chicken fast food chain of restaurants was founded by Colonel Harland Sanders when he was 62 years old, with only $105 in his pocket. Katsusuke Yanagisawa, who is a 71-year-old from Japan, reached the summit of Mount Everest, the highest mountain in the world.

Looking back in time, there are moving stories that illustrate this point further. In 1883, for instance, John A. Roebling and his son wanted to build a magnificent bridge in New York City that was considered impossible by the world bridge-building experts of the day. After his father's death, Washington Roebling remained inspired to complete the project despite an accident that left him with brain damage and unable to walk, talk or move, except for one finger. He used his one finger to tap a code on his wife's arm to give all the instructions to the engineers on how to complete The Brooklyn Bridge.

What is exciting to realize is that these were just people with a dream of something that they felt would make their lives more fulfilling. We all have different goals and aspirations. What sounds exciting and meaningful to one person may not be to another. However, what is important is knowing or revealing what feels meaningful to you. Throughout these pages you will be encouraged to clarify your desires and discover, or rediscover, your dreams.

Stepping Stones

Taking stepping stones to achieve your desires breaks down the process into manageable chunks, one step at a time. Although this may seem obvious it is often overlooked.

For example, if you are currently bedridden and want full health again, you may not actually believe that this is possible for you. In this situation you might see yourself being able to sit up in bed for a while every day. That might be an attainable and believable desire as a stepping stone towards your overall goal. Once achieved, the idea is to build on that success by setting your sights on another achievable goal such as being able to walk a few paces every morning with some help from a friend. Next the goal might be to walk slowly around your room unaided and so on. Everyone's situation is different but the idea is still the same; each little step in the right direction will take you to what want you want to achieve.

Releasing Resistance

A checklist of questions will be given for you to feel your way through. To identify and release any emotional blocks that might otherwise stop you from attaining your desires.

When you get to the point in Chapter 8 that explains how to start Surfing Rainbows and you are asked to go through the Releasing Resistance Checklist, it is worth taking the time to do this thoroughly, whether you take a few moments, a few days, a few weeks or a few months. When one of the points in the checklist flags up an issue that you do not feel one hundred percent happy with, then you will be directed to some notes which will help you release that resistance. It really does not matter how long it takes to go through this checklist, but it is absolutely imperative that you feel totally happy with each of the points raised by each question. This is important so that you fully release the emotional blocks that would otherwise be stopping you from attracting what you want into your life.

You may feel it useful to go through the Releasing Resistance Checklist a few times for each desire. With each time that you do, you will be clarifying your desire further and releasing more emotional blocks so that you will be attracting your desires to you faster.

If you become overwhelmed or confused at the amount of new desires that seem to pop up as you go through the Releasing Resistance Checklist, just remember that the purpose of the exercise is to clarify the detail of each main desire. The desires that pop up, which are linked to your main desires, help achieve this clarity.

You are not expected to sort everything out at once. Just do what feels good to you. You may like to look at all your desires as you go through the list, alternatively you may like to just focus on one desire at a time.

Creating Rainbow Expressions

Creating a Rainbow Expression is a means of becoming clearer about your desires and intensifying your feelings about them so that you attract them faster.

The process of experiencing something you don't want helps you identify what you do want.When you know what you want you can clarify this new desire, release any emotional blocks and discover what conditions you require to allow it into your life.

You only have to think about your desire once to attract it…but to keep attracting it until you receive it you need to keep your vibes high. So when you feel upset that you don't have your desire yet, you are repelling it, but when you focus on it with happy thoughts you are attracting it. Rainbow Expressing your desire helps you maintain the high vibes you need. The better you feel, the more your chakra two is in balance, the higher your vibes and the faster you are attracting all that you want.

Step 3

Surf Rainbows To Maintain Optimized Energy Levels

The Golden Intention Code

What is it?

The Golden Intention Code consists of a set of statements that are given in Chapter 8 (on page 106) for when you start Surfing Rainbows. As you read these statements, they give you instant accurate feedback on your flow of energy through your chakras. The statements also offer a Rainbow View of Life (an affirmation to maintain optimized energy levels in general) and a means of Rainbow Expressing your desires (a visualization to maintain optimized energy levels in relation to your desires).

The Golden Intention Code can also be used as a powerful guided meditation.

Why use it?

- To help you quickly identify which chakras are out of balance and where to readdress the balance
- To constantly raise the level of your good feelings to a new norm, as this helps you to attract your desires faster.
- To state your intention of how you want to feel during your day. This gives a very positive affirmation of what you want to attract into your life. As you continue to affirm The Golden Intention Code, what you read, and the desires you welcome, are indeed what you do attract into your life.

When to use it?

- Anytime you feel you need an energy boost or a pick-me-up.
- Aim to read The Golden Intention Code on waking in the morning and before going to sleep. Aim to make it something as habitual as brushing your teeth morning and night.
- Allow it to become a way of life; a code to live by.

Where to use it?

Anywhere you like. You can do it while you are out and about, or at home. If at home, you may like to do it in a quiet place, away from distractions and electrical devices such as televisions and computers. Aim to be consistent with this every day, whenever you decide the best time is for you.

A point worth mentioning is that the more you enjoy Surfing Rainbows at the beginning, the more you are likely to continue surfing, and the more proof you will have that it works. Therefore, in addition to saying The Golden Intention Code morning and night, you may also like to incorporate reading, or remembering it, when you are doing something you love doing, like sitting in your garden, walking in the park, jogging by a lake or relaxing in the bath.

Taking a Rainbow View of Life

What is it?

Taking a Rainbow View of Life means taking a perspective from moment-to-moment throughout your day that aims to optimize your energy levels.

Taking a Rainbow View means that you are:

- Trusting your feelings to make good decisions.
- Appreciating what you already have and persistently holding an optimistic perspective on any new desires that you would like to experience.

- Knowing that you deserve your desires and so you are allowing them into your life.
- Sensing whom to trust to open doors to new opportunities for you.
- Allowing your good feelings to guide your thoughts, words and actions, which positively shifts your energy levels throughout your day. This helps you stay optimistically focused on your target.
- Allowing yourself some time to relax every day. This helps you receive flashes of inspiration to fulfill your goals faster.
- Relaxing and enjoying life as each of your desires unfolds.

Why do it?

The main purpose is to harness the power of your intention. As you know, every thought that you think affects your feelings and stimulates your chakras in one way or another throughout your day. Negative thoughts make you feel drained and decrease your energy, whereas genuinely positive thoughts uplift you; they power you up and balance your chakras.

When you allow something that happens during your day to knock you flat emotionally, you have subconsciously made the choice to allow it to push you out of balance. The negative feelings coursing through your body limit your energy flow so that you block, rather than attract, your desires. The purpose of reading and living by The Golden Intention Code is to ensure that you stay in vibrational alignment. That is why it is suggested you read and live by it every day.

Each of the statements within The Golden Intention Code relates to one of the seven major chakras. When you read the statements, and check how you feel, you receive instant, accurate feedback on the flow of energy through each of your chakra energy valves.

When you are emotionally shut down, one or more of the seven chakra energy valves will also be shut down. Irrespective of the problem you are facing, at the core of the issue there will always be a feeling of lack in relation to one or more of the following areas:

- trust
- joy
- worthiness
- love
- positive expression
- inspiration
- enlightenment

This is why it is so important to check how you feel when you read the statements, as that helps you to identify where you may be emotionally shut down, and which chakra is out of balance. If you do not feel good when you read any of the statements, you will be directed to look at a few notes. The notes are aimed at reminding you of a more open mindset, to shift your mood, to optimize and to rebalance your energy. By becoming much more in tune with your feelings through Surfing Rainbows, you will quickly recognize whether or not your energy is in alignment and so whether or not you are fully benefiting from the Law of Attraction.

You may like to breathe deeply and slowly as you read The Golden Intention Code because this calms the racing mind and allows a sense of relaxation to be attached to the affirmation created when you read it.

Studies have shown that during meditation the "thinking mind" slows down and a deeper connection with one's inner wisdom and feelings occurs[11]. This is why the Golden Intention Code is also offered as a meditation.

You will see as you read the statements that you are also encouraged to feel glad about and grateful for what you already have. Try to focus on different things every day that you are grateful for. The grateful mind begins to expect good things and these expectations increase the belief that more good things will come your way. Independent studies by different researchers worldwide have shown that those who show gratitude every day have higher levels of happiness, optimism, alertness, determination, enthusiasm and energy than those who do not.[12]

---

11 *Dr. Gregg Jacobs, The Ancestral Mind, (available through amazon.com)*
12 Dr. Robert Emmons & Dr. Michael McCollough, *The Psychology of Gratitude*, 2004.

As you shift your focus from what you and others do not have and become more grateful for and appreciative of everything that you do have, this gives you a mindset of abundance. When you resonate with the vibe of abundance and appreciation, love and joy, your energy becomes more balanced and that attracts back more situations that make you feel just as good.

Rainbow Expressing Your Desires

What is it?

Rainbow Expressing is a powerful visualization technique to maintain optimized energy levels in relation to your daily and long term desires. This is a fun way of helping you become clearer and more excited about your desires. It can take as little as a few seconds, a few minutes, or as long as feels good. It asks you to specifically dwell on and absorb some wonderful thoughts and feelings to uplift you.

Consider three points of a triangle... ABC. If you are standing at point A and want to reach point B, but you are only allowed to look at point C, you will find it hard, if not impossible, to walk in a straight line to point B. It is much easier if you are looking where you are going and only focusing on your desired destination. That is what you are doing when you are Rainbow Expressing your desires.

Many people state what they want by talking about what they do not want. You will often hear it said, "I don't want that anymore because..." However, if you are aiming for a target and you are slightly off course, you will miss it. Looking at your desires in this way is very unhelpful because anything is much easier to reach when you focus directly on it.

So rather than stating that you want to be debt free, express that you want greater wealth. Likewise, rather than stating that you want to... stop taking drugs, stop smoking, stop excessive drinking or stop being a workaholic, you will find it much easier to break free from addictions if you use whatever words you find meaningful that convey freedom from the addiction itself.

Rainbow Expressing your desires consists of taking a moment to picture yourself having your desires and enjoying the feelings that this gives you. You may find it helps to imagine yourself looking at some photographs or watching a home movie that shows you already enjoying your desires, because by virtue of the fact you are picturing looking at photographs, you have to have the desires in your life already.

The National Academy of Sciences[13] noted that many Olympic Gold Medalists focus on their desired end goals and play the winning sequence they want to make their reality over and over again in their minds.

Breaking free of old mindsets may take a certain amount of determination, especially when old habits of thinking the same thoughts keep attracting the "same old...same old" experiences into your life, time and time again. However, if any doubts or concerns enter the minds of these Olympic Gold Medalists, for instance, they become so skilled at letting the negative thoughts go, they can simply change the images on the movie screens of their minds back to the detailed images of the performance they are aiming for.[14] Eventually, their desire becomes such a strong "intention to have" that they establish it as fact in their mind's eye. The power of intention, consciously choosing where to direct your thoughts, is a creative force that is enormous, and incredibly effective, which is why Olympic Gold Medalists use it.

Srinivasan Pillay, psychiatrist and brain imaging researcher at the McLean Hospital in Belmont, Massachusetts, describes how visualization has been proven to be effective in the recovery of stroke patients. After a stroke, where the blood clot occurred in an artery of the brain, the tissue that was once fed by that artery is starved of nutrients and therefore dies. This decay spreads. Research has shown that when the patient visualizes movement in the paralyzed limb, blood flow to the affected part of the brain is increased, which reduces the amount of tissue death, and therefore assists recovery. [15]

---

13 *Enhancing Human Performance: Issues, Theories, and Techniques,* Washington DC: National Academy Press 1988.
14 B.Rushall, Sport Psychologist, *Covert modelling as a procedure for altering an elite athlete's psychological state,* (1988) 2:131-140
15 Pillay, Srinivasan, *The Science of Visualization,* The Huffington Post, posted March 3, 2009

Other researchers have also concluded that the same method of mind imagery is effective for improving one's health.[16] This technique is equally effective if your goal is to run a successful business, pass your exams, be offered a job, conceive a baby or enjoy a wonderful home life.

Why do it?

The main purpose of Rainbow Expressing your desires is to harness the power of your intention. By expressing your desires a certain way you will achieve an "express" delivery of them.

There are so many reasons to Rainbow Express your desires, here are a few more:

- To intensify your feelings about your desires so that your vibes become stronger and you attract them faster.
- To help you see yourself as having your desires *NOW*, because if you think of them as being in your future, that is where they will stay...in your future.
- To clarify what conditions you need to have met to feel safe allowing your desire into your life. For example, you may want to have a successful business, but only under the condition that you have the full support of your family, and that the business grows at a steady pace so you can cope with it easily (otherwise you may prefer to stay in your current job).
- To check that you believe you can have your desire. If you do not believe your desire is possible, then you are blocking yourself from achieving it. The vibes you send out will be repelling your desire, rather than attracting it.

How often?

How often should you be Rainbow Expressing your desires? Rainbow Express them as often as feel good to you. If it feels good to Rainbow Express every now and again during your day, then do that. If it feels good to do it just

---

16 *Mind-body medicine: State of the science: Implications for practice.* J.A. Astin et al., Journal of the American Board of Family Practitioners, 2003; 16 (2):131-47

once or twice a day, then do so. And if it just feels great to do it once every few days, then that is fine too, because what is important is how good it feels to you when you do it.

However, as Rainbow Expressing helps you attract your desires a lot faster, it is worth finding ways of making this a fun thing for you to do so that you enjoy doing it and want to do it. Did you ever daydream as a child, and do you remember how wonderful that felt? Rainbow Expressing should feel equally wonderful and even more exciting, because it will indeed help you to be awake and aware when you experience your dreams!

Rainbow Expressing is a great pick-me-up if something happens during your day that upsets you. You will learn how to release the negative emotion about what has upset you, reverse the problem to state it as a desire and then refocus on your new desire and on what makes you feel good, so that your good feelings guide you to achieving it.

Chapter Summary

- The better you feel, the higher your energy levels, the better your vibes and the faster you attract your desires. This is what is happening when you are Surfing Rainbows as you take the following steps:

1. Optimize your energy levels in general
2. Optimize your energy levels in relation to your desires
3. Maintain optimized energy levels

Chapter 6

The Effectiveness of Surfing Rainbows

Your energy levels impact every area of your life, whether you are at work, home or play. For anyone who may still be uncertain, here are two very basic examples that are easy to relate to. When you fall in love and think about your new partner, you are likely to feel great. You are likely to be on a high and have high energy levels. Therefore you will be sending out wonderfully high vibes and attracting more good experiences back to you. That is, until you start focusing on things that bother you; then the downward spiral kicks in.

By contrast, if you lose your job and let yourself dwell on the anger you feel towards your boss, you will feel lousy, be on a downer, have low energy levels and therefore send out low vibes and attract more bad experiences back. That is, until you change your point of view, see past your current situation, release the emotional blocks and start doing things that make you feel good again. This breaks the cycle and helps you climb back up the spiral to attract better experiences to you.

Many people are in the habit of negative self-chat, putting themselves down and thinking thoughts that make them feel not so good about themselves. Rainbow Viewing and Rainbow Expressing help us change that habit.

As previously stated, in life we do not achieve what we are capable of, we achieve what we believe we are capable of, and it is the thoughts we think that set up these beliefs. When Rainbow Viewing and Rainbow Expressing regularly, we are affirming and thinking good thoughts about ourselves and our dreams and so we are setting up an empowering set of self-beliefs.

The more we think these good thoughts, the more we believe. The more we believe, the more we become convinced, and the more convinced we become, the faster we create. This is because the higher our vibes, the more we benefit from the Law of Attraction. So simple, so powerful, so effective.

For illustrations of Rainbow Expressions relating to the issues given below, please see the Examples & Notes on page 147.

Health Related Rainbow Expressions

Many of us have heard about people who have regained or improved their health against all probability. Making a much better recovery than expected after accidents or operations, they defy the odds and achieve health results that even the medical experts cannot account for. Indeed, there are cases of people who have been told they cannot conceive but do so. There have also been cases of people who have lived many years after they had been diagnosed with terminal cancer and given the prognosis of just a few months to live.

This is not stated to discredit the work of the medical experts, but rather to give examples of where people have shifted their emotional state and in so doing have allowed their bodies to heal naturally.

Both Brandon Bays and Louise Hay are well known examples of people who were diagnosed with large cancerous tumors and who embarked on their journey to release their negative emotional issues. They focused their minds on the health they wanted and were able to recover fully without much medical help.

When you envisage yourself as healthier, you start acting and behaving as someone who is healthy and this actually contributes to making you healthier. Indeed, scientists have confirmed the impact of a patient's outlook in the healing process.[17]

When you Rainbow Express your desires properly, you feel genuinely happy. Scientists have documented that when you laugh and feel good there are a number of physiological benefits to the body, including a reduction in the amount of stress hormones released into the bloodstream. This is important because, when the body is stressed it will slow down the nutrition sent to, and therefore the functioning of, the organs that are not vital to your immediate survival, and this includes the reproductive and main internal organs.

---

17 Van Baalen DC, et al., *Psychosocial correlates of 'spontaneous' regression of cancer.* Humane Medicine, April 1987.

Where someone desperately wants something (to conceive or to regain their health, for example) but an "expert" tells them that it is just not possible, the person may release the stress as they give up on their desire. They no longer centre their attention on it and their ensuing shift in focus onto other things may mean that the emotional block to their desire is also released. Often the person then easily achieves what they had wanted all along.

Most of us have heard about people who have let go of the struggle associated with wanting a family and have adopted children or given up on their fertility treatment, but then as their body relaxes they conceive naturally because their energy has come back into alignment.

Rainbow Expressions for a new home or a new job

When you picture in your mind's eye what your ideal home or job is like and you are excited about it, you are intentionally considering the aspects that will give you pleasure. This defines the area of your search and the requirements you would like to fulfill. Being clear about what you want and adjusting your outlook to encompass it increases your chances of attracting it.

Rainbow Expressions that relate to your work

If you keep focusing on things that annoy you at work, you will become even more annoyed. Many people are brought up to look for the pitfalls and to be careful and meticulous in scouring for problems before they arise. This cautious approach will sap your energy.

By taking on a more open and optimistic approach, you are releasing the possibilities for maximizing potential. When Surfing Rainbows you will feel genuinely positive, you are more relaxed and exude more confidence and this influences others to have more confidence in you. Consequently, you are more likely to be offered a job or given a promotion. Likewise, if your Rainbow Expression is for an expanding business network, this new attitude will encourage more people to join you; if it is improved sales figures that you are after then more people are much more likely to buy products from you because you appear genuinely happy and confident.

Rainbow Expressions for a loving relationship

When you are Surfing Rainbows you feel good. When you feel good you are naturally more fun to be around, while the opposite is true of someone who is feeling bad. By changing your outlook through Rainbow Expressing your desire you increase your vibrational rate and allow your energy levels to become balanced. When you give out higher vibes, you draw to yourself more positive events and people of a similar vibe, and this gives you the possibility of attracting more friends and finding a loving partner.

The desire to have a partner is the same whether you are feeling depressed, or whether you are feeling good within yourself; however the focus and shift in energy direction means that the vibes you send out are very different. This is a conscious choice. Rather than repelling what you want, you are attracting it.

Rainbow Expressions for improved relationships

When you are feeling resentful, angry or negative in any way, or if you miss the fun times you used to have with your partner, your partner will pick up on your vibes and will also become more negative. This is when you both tailspin down a negative spiral, both reflecting the pain that you feel. However, if instead you take a moment to look for all the little things that you used to love and appreciate about your partner, you will change your point of view and start feeling happier about why you are together. Your partner will eventually pick up and respond to your better mood, so that you will enjoy each other's company once again.

Rainbow Expressions are not a means of controlling others but they do control the situations that you attract to yourself, and they do influence others. As you change your own vibes by positively changing your outlook, you evoke the required qualities in either someone you already know or in someone new.

Again, this is *such a vital point to grasp:* if you have it in your mind that if someone or something has to happen for you to be happy, you are focusing on what you do not want, and so you are attracting more of the negative qualities that you would like to release. With Surfing Rainbows you begin to control what you pay attention to. This is significant because every thought impacts how you feel, and that controls what you attract into your life. So, when you have the vibe of being loving: you attract more love into your life.

Rainbow Expressions for "Impossible Dreams"

Rainbow Expressions clearly make sense when you consider common desires, but let us say you have a desire that your friends and family tell you is impossible. When you start Surfing Rainbows for this desire, it can still be yours.

The logical answer to why Rainbow Expressions will still deliver the results is because when you keep focused on a goal and keep heading towards it… little by little every day… you will eventually achieve it. Coincidences appear to happen and you feel inspired to take action. Even if you desire to achieve something that has never been done before, it is worth remembering that there will always be a first time for everything. There was a first time when someone walked on the moon, recovered from an illness that others said was incurable, climbed Mount Everest, etc.

When you are Rainbow Expressing your desires, you feel good about them. When you feel good, you are moving towards your desires, whereas when you feel bad your energy is repelling them.

Quantum physicists explain that everything is energy, with different energy vibrating at its own particular frequency. As like energy attracts like energy, vibrating energy of thought attracts the same frequency in matter.

Even if we do not understand the explanation the results speak for themselves. Rainbow Expressions deliver your desires; try and see for yourself! For many endorsements on the effectiveness of Surfing Rainbows please see page 195.

Expand what you believe; expand what you receive

Since you can receive into your life whatever you believe is possible, if you expand your beliefs, you can expand the abundance you are able to receive.

You may have based what you believe you can have on what you see others achieving. This may be a good starting point, but others may not be familiar with Surfing Rainbows and the importance of vibes for the delivery of desires, and so if you base your beliefs on those of others, then you are limiting your experience and what you believe you can achieve.

At one time everyone believed that the earth was flat, the sun revolved around the earth, we could cure a sick person by blood-letting, man would never be able to fly, mobile phones were impossible, telephone lines could not carry words and the internet would never become a reality. People believed these statements to be true, but now these beliefs have been superseded.

Beliefs are thoughts which you have had many times. Beliefs can be changed, modified and expanded; they can become empowering even from a limiting start.

Although you cannot push an old belief away, you can replace it. A belief is created by a thought that becomes fixed in your mind. Changing your point of view can allow you to change a belief that has become limiting. Intentionally choosing to adjust your outlook to a more positive, new perspective allows you to change a negative belief that you no longer need.

And as you begin to do this, you begin attracting more of the new thing you are thinking about and so your new belief begins to take shape.

The ramifications of your thoughts and beliefs were explained earlier by the example of navigating at sea. If you are off course by one degree, then you could be heading miles off target. A small margin of error makes a big impact on whether or not you reach your desired destination. Stop and think about this the next time you complain about the weather or get angry because you are stuck in a traffic jam.

By thinking about what you want and picturing yourself having it, by dwelling on why you want it and how that feels to you, you are creating new thoughts and new subconscious beliefs that help you focus in the right direction and help you head straight for your desires.

The Law of Attraction operates on the basis of like attracting like. If you want to connect with someone using a walky-talky or two-way radio, you have to be on the same wavelength. If you want to communicate with someone else on a different frequency, then you have to change the channels on the walky-talky so that you can make contact by sending and receiving on that new wavelength. Likewise, if you want to be able to receive different circumstances to those you are currently experiencing, you have to change the frequency that you are sending out.

You do not need to know how your desire will come into your life, just like you do not need to follow the chef in a restaurant back to his kitchen to find out how your meal will be cooked.

If you plant a flower seed, you know what you want the end result to look like and you believe it will grow and flower. You do not need to know how it grows, and if you doubt that it is growing and so keep digging it up to check that it is sprouting, then it is unlikely to grow as it should.

When you send out the best vibe possible, you attract any desire to you. That is *any* desire. So take the time to be grateful and really appreciate what you *do* have. Enjoy your life from moment to moment and be expectant in the same way as when you place an order in a restaurant. Keep your vibe high and your desire will soon be yours.

If it is really true that you can create anything you want, and you can, then why not give it a go? Why not go beyond your wildest dreams? Why not test this out?

But will the Good Luck Last?

When things start falling into place, life begins to flow and it is clear your desires are being drawn to you, you may start worrying whether your good "luck" will last. When you worry in this way, you stop trusting yourself and instead you start focusing on the lack of your desire again, so that is what you will begin attracting. Even though you had started to feel better (if improved health was your desire) or you met a wonderful person and started dating (if finding a new relationship was your desire) then in these examples, as you turn your attention and focus on what you do *NOT* want, your health may begin to deteriorate again and your date may not turn up next time.

There is great benefit in Surfing Rainbows every day even when things seem to be going well, because it helps ensure things *keep* going smoothly for you. As you keep in mind your next desire, and your next, and your next, they will keep unfolding the way you would like them to.

Chapter Summary

- When you genuinely feel good, which is what happens when you are Surfing Rainbows you attract all that you want because the wavelength you are on when you feel good is the same wavelength you will be on when you have your desires, which means you are taking maximum benefit from the Law of Attraction. This is why Surfing Rainbows is so effective.

Please visit
www.SurfingRainbows.com/Surfing
to see how effective other readers have been
in Surfing Rainbows for their desires.

Chapter 7

A Conclusion & A New Beginning

The person in charge of your happiness is you. If you could fast forward to the end of your life and look in the mirror, do you want to be looking back at someone who became resigned to a life of compromise, or do you want to be looking back at someone who reached for and achieved what they wanted?

If it is really true that you can create your future by choice rather than by chance (and you will have experience of this as you start Surfing Rainbows) then this is incredibly exciting! If it is also true that feeling good and having fun is the way to achieving your desires, then this should sound like a great plan.

Surfing Rainbows is all about identifying your desires and then enjoying them! It is about having a more fulfilling, abundant life with a lot less struggle! It is so simple and yet so effective! This is really something to be excited about!

Is there something that you have wanted for a long time? Is there a situation in your life at the moment that you want to improve? You may be asking yourself, "Can I really Surf Rainbows? Is it possible to do and will it work for me?" The real questions should be:

- Do I want my life to flow more easily?
- Do I want my desires enough for me to give this a proper try?

It is easy to let the fear of failure, the avoidance of disappointment, the feeling of not being good enough and so on, stop you from achieving your dreams and desires. It takes real character to change old habits and beliefs to try something new when others around you stick to their old ways. Even so it is possible and it is achievable.

How can this book help you? That depends on whether you are open to trying this wholeheartedly. If you are, then *The Promise of Surfing Rainbows* will help you absolutely.

Life is what you make it. Rather than putting this book back on the shelf with the others, why not try it out?

Have a go and start Surfing Rainbows…

Chapter Summary

- Surfing Rainbows holds the promise that once you start you will soon see results.
- You are also asked to make a promise, a promise to yourself to commit 100% to the 3 simple steps offered so that you will soon have all the evidence you need to to be sure that you are heading in the right direction to achieving your desires.

Part Two

How to start Surfing Rainbows!

Chapter 8

Start Surfing Rainbows!

We have discussed the WHAT, WHEN and WHY you are encouraged to Surf Rainbows, now we will explore HOW to start Surfing Rainbows.

There are three simple steps to Surfing Rainbows, and they are:

Step 1
Optimize Your Energy Levels in General
(The Feel-Good Lists, Energy Flow Chart & Improving Your
Self-Esteem Chart)

Step 2
Optimize Your Energy Levels in Relation to Your Desires
(Clarifying Desires, Stepping Stones, Releasing Resistance,
Creating Rainbow Expressions)

Step 3
Maintain Optimized Energy Levels
(The Golden Intention Code - Rainbow Viewing &
Rainbow Expressing)

Step 1

Surf Rainbows to Optimize Your Energy Levels in General

The Feel-Good Lists

You are encouraged to take a fresh sheet of paper for each of the lists that you are about to prepare. They will become your own valuable source of personal mood enhancing and energy boosting ideas that you can refer to, and add to, at any time.

When you feel terrible:

Although improving your mood is vital, sometimes it may seem incredibly difficult especially when you can't even think straight. Do you need to let off steam first? Take a moment to write down as many ways as you feel will help you do this. For example: 1) cry and shout, 2) go for a run, 3) punch pillows, 4) vent your random feelings in a letter that you then tear up.

The next time you feel really terrible, see which of your ideas works best for you to stop yourself from slipping further down the negative spiral.

When you feel bad:

The Feel-Good List that you are encouraged to complete now will be a useful resource for when you feel generally upset or anxious. On this new list jot down the things that help you forget about your worries for a while. Here are a few examples that have been successful for many: 1) watching a funny film, 2) playing sports, 3) looking at a joke or comic book, 4) stroking your cat / walking your dog, 5) dancing around your home to your favourite funky music, 6) taking a long, warm shower or bath, 7) flicking through some photos and reflecting on some good memories, 8) closing your eyes and imagining you are somewhere special.

Whenever you do feel quite low, refer back to this list. Keep trying different ideas and adding new ones. When your mood dips, be determined to keep focusing on things that make you feel better until you do actually begin to feel genuinely better. As you try out your different mood-enhancing ideas you will be shifting into a happier and more resourceful mindset and that will help you to start turning your situation around.

When you feel ready:

When you have shifted your mood sufficiently to think rationally, take a new piece of paper and draw a line down the middle of it. On the left hand side of the line, write down ALL the things that you don't like about the issue you are currently facing, and then on the right hand side of the paper, turn each point around to state what you would like to experience instead. Here is a simple example: My boss at work makes me so angry, he is always so rude and unfriendly / My boss is pleasant to work with and we have a good relationship.

The aim of this list is to help you start the process of clarifying your desires.

When you feel okay:

A lot of people are neither particularly happy, nor particularly unhappy about their lives. But, wouldn't it be wonderful to really love the life you live!

To begin to improve how good you feel about your life in general, make a list of all the things you do on a daily basis and rate how good you feel about each one. Next, have a think about the items that you have given a low score to and see how you can either change what you do or change how you feel about what you do. For example, if you hate the morning commute to work or tidying up your home, then look for ways to make this more fun and enjoyable. For some people this might mean listening to some comedy sketches in your car and it might mean tidying and cleaning your home while dancing and singing to music!

When you feel frustrated:

Remember that if you want to improve your life experiences, your vibes have to be high enough to attract what you want, and that means you have to feel good about the situation that you are currently in. This may seem extremely difficult and you could argue that if you felt good about your current situation you would not want to change it! However, you must change your mood if you want to change your situation.

List out what you can be grateful for in your life right now. If you want a better relationship, list and focus on the qualities you like in your various relationships. When you are ill, list out and focus on the parts of your body that are healthier, for example, you may still have your eyesight, you may have good hearing and you may have good strong teeth. Think thoughts that make you feel good about those things. This may all seem quite trivial but it is not. Every situation that seems awful, really awful, can somehow be looked at in a slightly better way. As you begin to feel better, your vibes will improve and so will your situation.

When you feel impatient:

This next Feel-Good List is going to serve as a really useful reminder when you feel impatient that you haven't yet achieved your desire. This list will help remind you of how far you have come on your journey to reaching what you want. So, list the milestones you have achieved on your journey to achieving your end goal and make sure that you keep this list updated as you reach and achieve your new desires.

Also, jot down a few more milestones that relate to your life in general, for example anything that you have achieved in your life to date, and what you should feel proud of.

When you want to feel great:

This next Feel-Good List is all about rediscovering the real you. Take another moment now to jot down what do you like and what don't you like. Make a note of the last time you had a really good laugh. What were you doing? Who were you with? Think of all the things that you used to really enjoy doing. Now see how you can introduce some things into your life that would give you the same good feelings that you enjoyed in the past. You can make a commitment to yourself to do one new thing from this list every week, or whenever it feels good to you to do so.

Here is an enlightening Feel-Good exercise to try every now and again. Close your eyes and imagine yourself meeting "you" as a child. Ask what "you" the child would like from "you" the adult to make it feel better. Perhaps "you" the child would like a hug, perhaps a chat over something upsetting or uplifting, or perhaps to play together. Spend a few moments with "you" the child; the "you" that is your inner child. Notice how good this makes you feel afterwards.

Energy Flow Chart

The Energy Flow Chart is another tool to help you feel hopeful and optimistic. The purpose of using the Energy Flow Chart is to help your thoughts focus on the progressively more positive aspects of an issue in order to improve your mood and balance your energy. This can be a quick or a very gradual process.

To complete the chart:

- Take a look at the list of feelings in the top left squares of the next Table. Scan downwards, looking for a feeling that best describes your current mood.

- Write down why you are feeling like that in the empty square next to it.

- Next, look further down the list and see if you can pinpoint another feeling that is also appropriate to the same situation. Just as you did before, make a note in the empty square next to it of the reasons why it could be appropriate and think about those reasons until your mood changes.

- You don't need to fill in all the empty boxes, just those that help you shift into a different mood. The idea is to keep focusing on thoughts and different feelings to help change your outlook. Initially this may mean dwelling on various different negative thoughts and emotions until you can shift yourself into finding more positive ones. It would be unrealistic to shift your mood from depression straight to elation, but with each shift in mood, you will be taking steps away from a powerless state of mind to a more empowered one.

- Keep working your way down the list, making notes in the empty column provided, so that by the end of the exercise you will have plenty of reasons why you should feel more hopeful and positive. This will serve as a valuable quick reminder and pick-me-up the next time you feel bad about by the same issue.

- You may need to work hard to find a new point of view. There may be issues that you find difficult to look at in a genuinely positive light, but shifting your point of view is essential because it releases emotional blocks.

- When you reach the mid-point in this chart you are asked to reverse your problem to see it as a desire. You can state what you DO NOT want and then turn it around to state what you DO want instead.

For extra support you can 'post your problem' and surf for the solution at **www.SurfingRainbows.com/Surfing**

Rainbow Energy Flow Chart	
A **List of Emotions**	**B** **Energy Alignment**
LOWEST FEELING / VIBES	
Fearful. Powerless, Despair, Desperate.	
Joyless. Envious, Resentful, Grieving, Depressed.	
Low Self-Worth, Low Self-Confidence. Self-pity, Insecure.	
Hatred. Angry, Revengeful, Distressed.	
Negative Self-Expression. Guilt, Aggravated, Annoyed.	
Uninspired. Confused, Disappointed, Discouraged, Overwhelmed.	
Unenlightened. Empty, Disinterested, Discontent.	
Reverse your problem to see it as a desire. Turn your desire into a Rainbow Expression. What can you feel encouraged and hopeful about?	
Trusting. Encouraged, Calm, Secure, Patient.	
Joyful. Cheerful, Aspire, Vision, Hopeful.	
High Self-Worth & Self-Confidence Determined, Eager.	
Love. Passionate, Certainty, Thrilled, Excited.	
Positive Self-Expression. Creative, Triumphant, Exhilarated, Enthusiastic.	
Inspired. Joyful Knowing, Clarity, Wonderment, Liberated	
Enlightened. Absolute Love, Total Appreciation, Pure Joy, Serene, Peaceful, Empowered, Fulfilled	
HIGHEST FEELING / VIBES	

This chart can help you improve your outlook as different issues arise in your life because it can be used in relation to anything you are thinking about. It encourages you to keep looking for ways to change your outlook so that your mood gradually keeps improving. For further clarity, there are some examples given on how to use the Chart in the Examples & Notes on page 115.

Even if you are in a bad mood but are not sure why, the Energy Flow Chart can still help you. Different issues may come to mind that you will able to discard there and then, or you may need to leave and return to them later.

From time to time you may like to check how good you feel about every aspect of your life, by rating it on a scale of 0-10. If anything needs improving use the Energy Flow Chart to turn it into a desire and then Surf Rainbows for it.

Feeling Safe and in Control

For anyone who feels uncomfortable with the idea of acknowledging their feelings, there is a method that can keep you firmly in control as you do any of the exercises offered: Picture yourself going into a room that you are familiar with and feel comfortable in. See yourself as being safe and happy in there. Now let the image of yourself, in your safe room, begin releasing the negative emotion through the methods described.

When you have finished releasing the negative emotion, picture the image of yourself leaving your safe room to join the physical you again. Throughout this process you have maintained full control and yet let go of an aspect of yourself that has been limiting your control over what you attract into your life.

Improving
Your Self-Esteem

On each row of the next Table you will find an exercise that is aimed at helping you improve your self-esteem, which impacts your energy levels. Take your time and go at your own pace. Enjoy the exercises and come back to them over and over again until you really feel great about how you answer each one.

Improving Your Self-Esteem	
If Only.../When I Have	Consider what there is about yourself that you would like to be different and complete the sentence, "If only I had ......then I could find / enjoy..." (for example "If only I had a better education then I could find a job easily." "If only I had longer legs and nicer hair, then I could find a partner easily." "If only a particular situation had or had not happened in my life..." "If only someone had, or had not said something..." "If only someone had, or had not done something...") Next complete the sentence, "When I have...then I..." (for example, "When I have a better job, then I can get a new car"). Write down as many "If only's..." and "When I have's" that you believe apply to you and then take each one in turn and reflect on it for a moment. Think about all the millions of people who have the same issues as you but who are enjoying the same things you desire. If others have the same issues as you but they are enjoying the same desires that you would like...then can you see that it should be possible for you to have them too?

(continues)

Releasing The Hurt	When you actually hear yourself saying your "if only," can you feel that you are allowing yourself to be pushed out of balance by it? Can you see that it is your choice how you view it? You can blow it up into something big and bad that continues to affect and hurt you deeply, or you can reduce it to an insignificant little thing and then move on.

Without condoning or even trying to understand anyone else's behaviour that you feel is the reason for you feeling bad about yourself, can you see that the person who is being hurt is you? If you now desire to release this past event or thought about yourself, so that you begin to feel better about yourself, then state the problem, which is how you feel, then reverse it and state how you would like to feel. This becomes a new desire. For more ideas on how to release the hurt see Note 23 in the Examples & Notes on page 142. |
| **Your Response** | Look back at that "if only" list you have just jotted down and remember the people who had those same issues but still achieved their desires.

Now imagine a few of your closest friends sitting with you. They are telling you that they have the same things on their list that make them think they are unworthy of having their desires.

What would you now tell your friends? |
| **Self-deprecating** | Notice how often you put yourself down during the day. If someone compliments you, can you accept it and say thank you or do you feel awkward? When you respect yourself more, others will respect you more. When you devalue yourself less and so value yourself more, so will others. |
| **Compliments** | Try to accept compliments from now on and avoid putting yourself down. Think of compliments that you have been given in the past and jot them down. Try to accept them, feel good about them and dwell on those good feelings. |

(continues)

Looking Ahead	Today you are creating your future, and the past will only hold you back if you let it. If you have done something that you are not proud of, know that it is in your past and start being more concerned with your "now." Don't keep judging yourself and putting yourself down, or others will too. No one has led a perfect life. Wipe the slate clean and start again. You have free will to change your thoughts and when you do, you will change your world.
Looking Good	How good we feel about ourselves on the inside is often reflected by how good we feel about ourselves on the outside.
	Do you like your hairstyle / clothes? Do you only have clothes in your wardrobe that you feel good in and like wearing? If there is anything that does not make you feel good when you wear it, is it time to give it away and replace it with clothes that do make you feel good?
Allowing of others	When you allow others to be themselves without criticizing them, you will find it easier to be more accepting and forgiving of yourself as well. You will also not be quite so bothered about what others think of you.
	Think of a few of the people you have recently judged in a bad light. It is very unlikely that you could have known all the background leading to the event that you judged.
	Let us take the example of a woman with a baby in her arms being jostled as she walked along a pavement; both she and the baby were fine. She was scared and furious with the man who had rushed passed her. She judged the situation as it occurred to her at the moment she was bumped into. However, there was no way that she could have known that the man had just received a phone call with urgent news of a family member who desperately needed him to go home.
	It is better not to judge others. You do not know their situation and when you become involved in angry thoughts, you are lowering your vibration and attracting more bad things you do not want. The person you hurt is yourself.

(continues)

Your Best Care	Imagine opening a door and seeing a little child alone in a room crying. This child is crying because all it wants is to be loved and yet all it receives is judgment and criticism.
	Are you treating yourself in the same way that this little child is being treated?
	Stop the negative self-talk and start loving yourself now. You deserve it, you always have.
	Why not start a new relationship with yourself today? Have you ever really stopped to question what you like and what you enjoy most in your day-to-day life? What do you like least? Explore the real you. Discover what makes you unique.
Your best friend	Instead of being your biggest enemy, become your best friend.
	There is no point in worrying about winning anyone else's approval. If you do not approve of yourself, others won't either. When you finally do give yourself approval, and therefore do feel good about yourself, the natural result is that you will attract others who will also approve of you.
Your Best feature	If you see a flower with half of one of its petals missing, it is still a beautiful flower, perfect in its imperfection. That is what makes it so unique. It would be very dull if all flowers were the same.
	Are you comparing yourself to computer-perfected models? Look around you when you are out and about; how many people actually look like that?
	Rather than focusing on the parts of you that you would like improved, decide what your best feature is, or your best few features, and focus on those.
	Everyone has different talents unique to themselves. Usually we are good at what we enjoy most. What are these things for you? Dwell on those things rather than the things you don't enjoy and are not so good at.

(continues)

| Make yourself important to YOU | Every day make *YOU* more important to yourself. Begin to like yourself more by loving and appreciating every aspect of your being. Take something different about yourself every day and appreciate it. Think of things that you can feel fortunate about and then dwell on those good feelings!

List some of the things that you should be proud of, that you have achieved and should feel good about. Tell yourself that you are unique and say why. There is no one like you in the whole world. Tell yourself that you love yourself and that you will start looking after yourself more and that you are worthy of any desire you choose to have! If you find this exercise hard to do, keep doing it every day until you really believe it. The more you feel love for yourself, the more you will attract others who will love you too. Look at yourself in the mirror and look into your eyes. Tell yourself that you love yourself and that you deserve all the richness that life has to offer. |

For more ideas on this please
visit our online workshop at
www.SurfingRainbows.com/Surfing

Step 2

Surf Rainbows to Optimize Your Energy Levels in relation to Your Desires

Clarifying Your Desires

You may be very clear about a desire that you want, and if this is the case focus on that one desire as you read on. However, if you want to take a broader perspective then take each area of your life in turn (health, money, family, friends, job, career, car, house, clothes, safety, security, etc.) and ask yourself how you feel your life could be improved.

- What would make your life so much better and more exciting, and why?
- Have you fulfilled your childhood dreams yet? Do you want to?
- What are the top five highlights of your life so far?
- Would you like to enjoy more experiences that would give you those same wonderful feelings?

Think past *any* obstacles that might seem to be in your way and uncover your deepest desires by spending a few more moments to consider what you would really like to happen and what you would really like to be, do, or have, if you knew that:

- You could not fail,
- You are able to face any fears,
- You have all the time and money you need, and
- Everything about the situation is now ideal for your desire to be fulfilled.

Have fun and scribble away, letting your imagination run wild.

Next, take a look at the desires that relate to each area of your life and put a time frame within which you would like to achieve each of those desires. Then, choose your most exciting desires and jot down ten reasons why you want them. Reflect for a moment on how your life would be if you did have them!

Now rate how much you really want each desire on a scale of 0-10. The stronger you feel about a desire, the more you will be drawn to achieving it.

Your Desires
Example: Be in a loving relationship. Earn more. Have a new home. Pass my exams.

This is a good time to be reminded that you do *NOT* have to know how your desires will come about because the answers will be revealed as you follow your good feelings, the inspiration that you receive and the coincidences that you will be drawn to. It is like driving a car in a new town; you may not know the road ahead, but if you follow the signposts they will lead you to your destination.

Remember whatever you want can come to you from loads of different sources. You're not supposed to work out how your desires will come about; all you have to do is follow your feelings so that they can and will come about!

Let us stop and take a moment. How are you feeling right now? We have reached a very exciting part of the book, because the next exercises are designed to help you release any emotional issues that may be holding you back.

If the thought of facing such issues seems overwhelming and your energy has dropped, then you might like to take a break and come back to the exercises when you feel rested and ready. Take a deep slow breath, all is well. Rather than use your mind as you run through the following exercises, trust the inner guidance of your feelings so that the emotional blocks can simply melt away.

Take Stepping Stones

Check how you feel about each of the desires you have listed. Do they feel like they are within reach or do you need some stepping stones? This is such a simple idea that it is so often overlooked, but it is also very important. Take a moment to consider if stepping stones to your end goal may make it seem easier for you to achieve. If you would like to skim through a few examples to see how to apply this idea to your own desires, you will find them in the Example & Notes on page 121.

Releasing Resistance

Run through the following checklist to release any resistance in relation to your desires. All the questions aim to reveal any emotional issues that may be affecting your seven chakras. Answer the questions from the perspective of how you are feeling right now, because that will pick up the emotional blocks that you have at this moment, and it is those that you are looking to release.

It is worthwhile going through this exercise when you are in different moods, because that may bring up different thoughts, different emotions and different blocks that also need releasing.

As you run through the checklist, ask yourself if you feel good or bad about any of the answers you give. If you do not feel very good about any of them, then stop and take a look at the corresponding points that are given in the Example & Notes section on page 124. Reflect on any issues raised until you definitely feel good about each one. You may find writing down the answers or talking them over with a friend may also be a way of helping you begin to feel better about the issues raised.

While you are welcome to read all the corresponding notes in the Example & Notes on page 124, you only need to read those that you feel are relevant to you at this time.

Releasing Resistance Checklist

Am I crystal clear about what I want? (See Note 1)
Am I clear about what steps I should take towards achieving my desire? (See Note 2)
Do I really want this desire for me? (See Note 3)
Is the desire really mine? (See Note 4)
Am I worried about being able to handle any problems that may arise as a result of my desire being fulfilled? (See Note 5)
Do I have the time to allow my desire into my life now? (See Note 6)
Do I feel safe, at this moment right now, allowing this desire into my life? (See Note 7)
When I think about my desire, do I hear myself saying "I can't have that because ..."? (See Note 8)
If my desire is achieved, what might I have to face that may bother me? (See Note 9)
Have I wanted something for a long time but not found the motivation or inspiration to go after it? (See Note 10)
Do I feel good, bad or ambivalent about the situation that I am in now? (See Note 11)
When asked, "Why do I have this desire?" Does the answer make me feel good or bad, or ambivalent? (See Note 12)
When I get in a panicked, stressed state about things, do I divert my attention immediately by changing my point of view? (See Note 13)
Do I always look for a better point of view? (See Note 14)
Do I believe that I can have my desire? (See Note 15)
Can I have this desire now, or does something else have to happen first? (See Note 16)
Can I picture myself enjoying my desire? (See Note 17)
Do I worry about what others will think of me if I have my desire? (See Note 18)
Am I open to being loving and do I encourage good relationships? (See Note 19)
Do I only focus on the desire I *DO* want rather than on what I *DO NOT* want? (See Note 20)
Do I take time to relax a little everyday? (See Note 21)
Do I enjoy my day knowing that my desires are unfolding? (See Note 22)
Do I always go through the process of minimizing thoughts and memories that upset me and maximizing thoughts and memories that uplift me? (See Note 23)

Turning Your Desires into Rainbow Expressions

All your desires now need to be turned into Rainbow Expressions by defining them by what you want, rather than by what you do not want. This is so important as whatever you focus on, you attract into your life.

You are about to review some of the thoughts you have had about your desires, and as you answer the following questions your Rainbow Expressions will come to light.

Take each of your desires in turn and run through these questions (if, as you are focusing on one desire, thoughts about different desires come to mind, just make a note of them on a fresh page to come back to later, so that you can keep focused on each desire in turn).

What is your desire?

If you haven't already done so, please write down your answer(s) to the question: What is your desire? The way you express your desire is very important because if your focus is remotely negative then those thoughts will be taking you off course. When you turn those thoughts around and you state your desire in more positive terms they can become positive, empowering affirmations of intention that feel great to you when you think about them.

For example, rather than saying I don't want to be in pain and constantly ill anymore, express your desire as feeling very well and being able to do the things that you want. For more examples in relation to other desires please see page 147.

What is the detail of your desire?

Again, if you haven't already done this, take a moment now to fill a whole page with the aspects and qualities of your desire. In other words what does your desire really mean to you, and what would make up your ideal scenario?

If your desire is a new house, then list out as much detail about it as you can. How many rooms does it have? What type of area is it in, etc? This will give you much more clarity and help you focus on what it is that you want and what excites you about your desire.

Remember do not try to work out how your desire is going to be fulfilled, e.g. you want a new job but only in that company, you want a new partner but only with the man you met at the bar last week, you want a new home and it has to be the one you visited yesterday. You do not need to work out how your desire will come about, just be clear on the specifics of how it will feel when it does come about because then you will be open to potentially better options.

Do you need some stepping stones?

Now let's double check that your desire still feels achievable. Check to see if you still feel good, or has your energy dropped? If your energy has dropped, this could be because your body is telling you that your desires feel unattainable and as that thought does not feel good, your chakras have closed a little and that makes you feel drained.

If this seems to be the case, you may need some stepping stones to take you to your end goal. For example, if the overall desire is that you want greater wealth, then a few stepping stones towards this may be: A) to have enough money to pay your immediate bills easily, B) then to have a steady source of income, C) then to have some money to spend on some treats, D) then to buy a new car, etc. For more examples of stepping stones in relation to different desires please see page 121.

What conditions do you need to feel safe?

Jot down the conditions that you have come up with (if any) that you need to have satisfied in order to feel safe allowing your desire into your life. Make a note of all the conditions attached to your stepping stones and also to your end goal as well. You may want to be in a loving relationship, for instance, but only if your partner is respectful, faithful and kind to you (otherwise you may prefer to stay single). For more examples please see page 148.

Why do you have this desire?

Try to fill a full page with plenty of reasons why you have this desire. Remember to stay positive. For every reason that you write down, ask yourself why that would be so good? This will give you even more reasons to feel good.

Think about how your life would improve when you have this desire fulfilled, as this will help you come up with even more reasons as to why you want it.

When you think of achieving this desire, how does it make you feel?

When you think about yourself enjoying your desire achieved, if something doesn't feel good then go back through the Surfing Rainbows Steps 1 and 2 again to see which emotional block needs releasing.

However, if the thought of enjoying your desire achieved does make you feel fantastic, try to think of a time when you have felt that good before, and write down what had just happened to make you feel so good. This could be something as simple as drawing a picture that you were really proud of, or passing an exam, going on your first date, receiving the keys to your new home, or it could be absolutely anything else that made you feel great.

Creating Your Rainbow Expression

Your Rainbow Expression is about to be created, and this is a very exciting moment. As a picture paints a thousand words, think of an image that would symbolize you achieving your new desire, with all your conditions met.

Here are a few examples: Opening an envelope and seeing your job acceptance letter! Being given the keys to your new home! Holding your new bank statement showing greater financial wealth! Perfect body weight may be looking down at the number on the scale that pleases you! Holding your healthy baby in your arms! Strolling in the park and enjoying your first kiss with the love of your life!

It is also very important to see all your conditions being met. So in the example where the desire is to be in a loving relationship and the condition is that you only want this if your partner is respectful, faithful and kind to you (otherwise you may prefer to stay single) then picture yourself with your partner doing something that symbolizes this respectful, faithful and kind attitude towards you.

Now imagine yourself looking at a few photographs with the image that symbolizes you achieving your new desire with your conditions being met. Imagine yourself stepping into the photos and enjoying all the good feelings that you want to experience. This is how you Rainbow Express your desire.

Have fun with imagining yourself enjoying your desires because the more fun you have, the better you will feel, the higher your vibes and the quicker you attract all that you want. You may find it easier to see yourself enjoying your desires somewhere that you are already very familiar with. You could be in your garden, at your local park, in your kitchen or amongst friends that you know well.

As your vibes are strongest when you are actually enjoying something, rather than thinking about enjoying your desire sometime in your future, look at your photos, or movie screen, showing yourself enjoying your desires now. Step into the photos or movie screen and enjoy those great feelings. When you think of yourself in the photos, try to involve all your senses. Let us take the example of holding the key to your new home. You could enjoy the image of holding the key and then running your hand admiringly over the new front door, smelling the fresh aroma of cooking and hearing your partner welcoming you as you step inside, perhaps you hear some music you like in the background.

Make the colours you imagine vivid and the sounds you are imagining become louder. Turn up the volume of the music you picture yourself playing when you are celebrating your success. Think back to the last time you really did feel this good and bring all those great feelings to you now.

Have fun creating your own visual
Rainbow Expressions online at
www.SurfingRainbows.com/Surfing

Step 3

Surf Rainbows to Maintain Optimized Energy Levels

The Golden Intention Code

The Golden Intention Code is the set of statements that give you instant accurate feedback on your energy flow.

The statements also offer you a Rainbow View of Life (an affirmation to maintain optimized energy levels in general) and a means of Rainbow Expressing your desires (a visualization to maintain optimized energy levels in relation to your desires).

By using The Golden Intention Code you generate the feelings within you that open your chakras, balance your energy, raise your vibes and so help you fully benefit from the Law of Attraction.

For a greater understanding of the value of
The Golden Intention Code please visit
www.SurfingRainbows.com/Surfing

The Golden Intention Code Unleash Your Energy, Unleash Your Life	Chakra
I feel safe trusting my feelings to make good decisions and to guide me to achieving my desires.	1
The things in my life that make me happy are…*(think about a few of them now)*	2
Rainbow Express your desires.	2
I am unique and special. Everyone, including me, deserves to be happy and enjoy a good life. *(Reflect on something you have done ,or something about yourself that makes you feel good)*	3
The things in my life that I love are…*(think about a few of them now)*	4
I love myself. I am happy to give, receive and be surrounded by love.	4
I constantly shift and direct my thoughts, words and actions onto what feels good so that I always feel good.	5
As I relax today I welcome clarity and inspiration.	6
I enjoy my day, and the unfolding adventures of my life!	7

How to Crack The Golden Intention Code: Basic Instructions

Taking a Rainbow View

- Relax, breathe deeply and read The Golden Intention Code on waking in the morning and before going to sleep (or whenever else feels good to you).
- Make sure that you feel good and agree with each statement.*
- Dwell on all the uplifting feelings the statements give you because that is what balances your chakras.

*Note: If you do not feel good about any of the statements, then something in your day, or in your thoughts overnight, has shut you down emotionally and one of your chakras needs to be balanced to readdress the energy flow again. There are various ways you can release the resistance. Start by looking at the corresponding notes given in the Quick Reminders on page 154. Also pick any of the exercises from Steps 1 and/or 2 that you feel may be appropriate. You will know when you have readdressed the energy balance and the resistance has gone because you will feel good when you come back and reread the statements of The Golden Intention Code.

If you understand the reasoning behind the statements and want them to be true but find them hard to say, you may need some stepping stones again. For example, one of the statements relating to Chakra Four is "I love myself." If you do want to love yourself but you do not feel that way yet, you can modify the statement so that you feel comfortable.

In this example you could say something like, "my intention is to love myself," "day by day I am learning to love myself more," or "I treat myself with loving kindness." As your fourth chakra begins to open up more and as the days go by, you will eventually feel comfortable saying what is written in the Golden Intention Code, "I love myself," and at that point, you will know that your fourth chakra is more open.

Rainbow Expressing Your Desires

Within the Golden Intention Code you are asked to Rainbow Express your desires.

- Rainbow Expressing your desire simply means enjoying the great feelings that you have when you picture yourself looking at a few photographs showing you achieving your new desires with all your conditions being met. You can imagine stepping into the photos and really enjoying the experience. It can take you a couple of seconds, minutes or you can do it for as long as you like.
- Take a moment to breathe in and relax, imagining yourself absorbing all those good feelings into your body.*
- When you Rainbow Express in the morning, remember to think about what you want to achieve and enjoy during your day as well, and then dwell on the good feelings that would give you.
- As you finish The Golden Intention Code, consciously decide to feel open to attracting the desires you have just pictured or something even better.

*Note: If you do not feel good when you are Rainbow Expressing your desires then go back and run through Steps 1 and 2 again until you do feel good.

Remember, if you feel good when you are picturing enjoying your desires, then you are attracting them. If you feel bad, then you are repelling them. The simple check to confirm if you are attracting rather than repelling your desire is given by your answer to how good you feel about it on a scale of 0 – 10 (where 0 is terrible and 10 is fabulous). The better your answers make you feel, the faster you are attracting your desire to you.

You may find after a few days of Rainbow Expressing a new desire it becomes hard to do or you can picture yourself enjoying part of your desire but not all of it. When this happens, go back and run through Steps 1 and 2 again with the part of the desire that feels blocked to you, because your subconscious mind may have unearthed a new hidden belief or a new condition that needs to be addressed as it is holding you back from allowing your desire into your life.

It may be that this process will happen a few times for each desire. With each time it does, you will be clarifying your desire further and revealing and releasing more emotional blocks so that you can attract what you want to you faster.

How to Crack The Golden Intention Code: Advanced Instructions

Taking a Rainbow View

You may like to take The Golden Intention Code one stage further by doing the following as you read the statements:

- Imagine that you are breathing in sparkling white* light. Imagine it filling up your arms, your legs, torso and head as well as the space around you. Bring all your attention to your various body parts as you imagine them filling up with white light. Imagine it cleansing, refreshing and energizing you.

- Breathe deeply, take as many, or as few breaths as you want, embracing various wonderful, uplifting feelings. You can either think of the uplifting feelings associated with each chakra, or think of a time when you felt most loved and loving, and absorb those feelings.

- You can send the light and loving uplifting feelings to every cell of your body, to the child within you, to an area of your life you want to improve, or an area of your health that you want to improve.

- This can be a quick or a long process; whatever feels good to you. It is a wonderful way to help keep all your chakras in balance.

*Note: Basic physics states that the colour white is the mix of all the colours from the rainbow. For centuries, ancient knowledge has referred to the "healing white light" because it is the total mix of all the colours that resonate within the body's chakra energy system when healthy and in balance.

Again, you do not have to, but you may like to take The Golden Intention Code one stage further again by doing the following as you read the statements:

- Do the same as above, but this time rather than breathing in the white light, breathe in the corresponding colour that is associated with each chakra**. You can also imagine being refreshed and cleansed by energized coloured droplets of water in a Rainbow Shower. You may like to try this when you are actually having your daily bath or shower. Imagine the water as liquid light to heighten your experience. If you love being outside in the park and surrounded by flowers, by the sea walking on the sand, or being somewhere or doing something else, then you may also like to imagine yourself having your Rainbow Shower there.

- When you really get into the swing of how amazing this process is and you really feel the power of what you are doing, then you may like to embrace The Golden Intention Code with even greater enthusiasm. For example, you may like to change the words relating to chakra one by stating something like this...I feel totally safe allowing my feelings to guide me. With chakra two... I feel abundant joy in my life! etc.

**Note: Chakra 1 = Red. 2 = Orange. 3 = Yellow. 4 = Green. 5 = Blue. 6 = Indigo. 7 = Purple / White.

Rainbow Expressing Your Desires

The next Table offers an overall understanding of the most effective ways of thinking about your desires to encourage great feelings about them.

Everyone Rainbow Expressing their desires will find the information in the Table useful and effective, so it is worth referring to them now and again as a general reminder on the ideas given. If you would like to take a more advanced approach to Rainbow Expressing your desires then aim to make a definite habit of using the techniques explained as often as feels good to you.

Rainbow Expressing

Refer to this list regularly to refresh your mind on how to Rainbow Express your desires

Your Conditions

You may be able to picture your conditions being satisfied while you are seeing yourself enjoying your desire, or this may still be too big a step for you. In that case see your condition being met first, then see yourself walking into a new space, perhaps through a door. Your condition is now met and now you are in a safe place, ready to see yourself enjoying your desire.

Play Some Music

Music is a very powerful tool. When you are Rainbow Expressing your desires, you may want to enjoy some music that gives you the same high, the same wonderful feeling that you know you will have when you are actually celebrating the enjoyment of your desire.

Sense Your Desire More

To jump into the feelings and excitement of seeing yourself achieving your desires, you may find that if your desire is a new home or new car, for example, it may help you to see a brochure or photo of the car or type of house you want.

If you enjoy the sense of taste, then you could imagine dining at your favorite restaurant to celebrate the new job you want.

Another possibility when you are watching your home movie is to imagine yourself hearing a piece of music that you will play to celebrate your success.

Remember The Time

If your desire is for success, then remember a time and place when you achieved something you are very proud of and then keep dwelling on how good you felt then and how that would feel to you now. If your desire is for greater health, then remember a time and place when you did have greater health. See yourself as you were then and keep dwelling on how good you felt then and how that would feel to you now. Likewise, if your desire is for more wealth, remember the time when you came across some money, etc.

(continues)

Expand The Feeling

For example, if you want a successful business, take the thought of being successful in some other area of your life and then expand that feeling of success to your business. If you want to have a body which is pain free and yet you are currently in a lot of pain, take a part of your body, such as your finger, where you have no pain and then expand that feeling of comfort to the rest of your body. If you want more wealth but you have so many bills that you cannot pay, take the thought of having a wealth of love, of water, of anything, and then expand that feeling of wealth to your finances. Likewise, if you want a new wonderful relationship, take the thought of your wonderful relationship with your friends, your pet or your neighbour and then expand that feeling to having a new wonderful relationship with a new partner.

See New Photos or a New Home Movie

Change what you see on your photos or home movie often, to keep it exciting to you.

Zoom In

Zoom in and focus on one part of the photo and then another part.

Stay Open Minded

Remember, do not fix your mind on how to solve a problem because you will become closed to potentially more appropriate options. For example, instead of wanting a relationship with one particular person, when there are potentially better matches, focus on the qualities and the essence of what you want from your dream relationships, your dream jobs, your dream house etc. Be open to allowing something even better to be attracted to you.

What's Next?

If you are Rainbow Expressing for a new partner, then imagine some of the things you would be doing together after you have met. If you are Rainbow Expressing for greater health, then imagine some of the things you will do when you are better. By doing this, you are directing how you would like your life to flow after your desire has been achieved. Really get into the feel of how great that is!

And For Today?

Run through the things that you would most like to do / enjoy / accomplish today. See yourself flicking through a few more photographs depicting yourself enjoying these desires as well. You can rate each desire from 0-10 to check your feelings in relation to them.

As you start making a habit of optimizing your energy, you will know you have mastered Surfing Rainbows because your desires will be effortlessly fulfilled. You will come to see that, as your current desires are evolving every day and as you can create new ones as well, you can indeed relax and enjoy a fun, worry-free day...every day.

Keep a list of all the desires that you bring to yourself via Surfing Rainbows. As this list becomes longer and longer, it should give you more and more confidence to keep on Surfing Rainbows to attract the very best that life has to offer!

Chapter Summary

- You can tell if you are Surfing Rainbows and therefore taking maximum benefit from the Law of Attraction by how good you feel on a moment-to-moment basis throughout your day.
- Feelings are an effective indicator as to the direction you are heading on the up/down spiral of life experiences. So welcome all your feelings both positive and negative and then take note of the accurate guidance from this natural internal intelligence.

Visit **www.SurfingRainbows.com/Surfing**
where you can freely express yourself.
Try out the 'venting corner' when
you need to let off steam!

Chapter 9

Examples & Notes

Using the Energy Flow Chart

The Energy Flow Chart is pivotal to Surfing Rainbows. Although you may not be able to relate to the issues discussed in the examples below, the examples are offered to give you a feel for how to apply the Energy Flow Chart to your own dilemmas.

Example: Money worries

I have bills to pay and no money to pay them with. I feel desperate. I find where desperate is on the Energy Flow Chart and then look for a way of viewing my situation slightly differently, by working my way down the list of emotions for a better feeling.

Well, even if I don't admit it openly, now and again I do feel a little resentment and anger because others seem to have plenty of money when I don't. As I look down again, I see discontent. Yes I certainly feel that.

As I keep looking down, I see the word "encouraged." What can I feel encouraged about? Well, I could be receiving more work soon. I could find other work as well. A big project may be underway soon. Yes, I could feel a little encouraged. I dwell on that feeling for a moment. I do feel a bit better.

I'm ready to keep working my way through the issue to see what other emotion could now be appropriate. I see the word "self-confident." What can I feel self-confident about?! Well, I am very good at what I do. I have had many compliments by lots of people. Yes I should feel good about myself. I should receive more work. I should earn more money!

I see the word "determined" on the chart. Yes I do feel more determined. I want a life where money is easy. I do deserve that! Next, I see the words "love" and "passionate." I feel great when I am involved in a certain type of work; it really fires me up.

I'm ready to turn my worry into a desire and my desire would be to have enough money to pay my bills and do other things too! So I could Rainbow Express for doing more of the type of work that really excites me; work that I really enjoy. Now I feel strong enough and hopeful enough to reverse my problem and state it as a desire. I Rainbow Express my new desire and take a Rainbow View. I feel a lot better; I feel a lot more hopeful.

I scribble down the thought process I just went through, and I keep it in my pocket so the next time I feel desperately low again, I can look at all my comments to keep myself feeling genuinely more positive about my desire, which I shall Rainbow Express every day until it comes into my life. Even then, I will continue to Rainbow Express for it, so that I continue to have enough money.

Example: Health worries

I have so many aches and pains. The doctors don't know what is wrong with me and I am sick of being ill. I feel very afraid.

I find where feeling fearful is on the chart and look down the chart for a stronger emotion. Yes I feel insecure and powerless! My doctor told me that he cannot help me and that I have to get used to all this pain! Yes I can feel anger! Why should I have to get used to it?!

I look further down, and I see the word "confused." Yes I feel confused! I am receiving so much conflicting advice; what am I supposed to do?! And yes I feel disappointed because no one knows what is wrong with me and I am in such pain all the time. I keep looking down the chart, and I see the word "hopeful." I guess there is a glimmer of hope. I have been in a lot of pain before with other things and the pain did pass and I did get better. Next I see the word "determined." What do I have to feel determined about? Well, I would like to enjoy the party I am organizing! I would like to be well enough to dance and have fun. Wouldn't that be just fantastic!

So if I turn my worry into a desire, it would be to have better health so that I can enjoy my friends and enjoy my party! All right, next I see the word "enthusiastic." What on earth do I have to be enthusiastic about? Ah yes, the Doctors did mention they had a new test they wanted to do. Maybe that will give them some direction and I could try the alternative therapy my friend was talking about.

Now I feel strong enough and hopeful enough to reverse my problem and state it as a desire. I Rainbow Express my new desire and take a Rainbow View. I feel much better and a lot more hopeful.

I complete the chart with all these and more of my comments, and I keep it in my pocket. The next time I feel afraid and panicky again, I can look at all my comments and keep myself feeling genuinely more positive about my desire. I shall Rainbow Express every day until it comes into my life. Even then, I will continue to Rainbow Express for it, so that I continue to have much better health.

Example: Wanting a Partner

Now an example is given using the Energy Flow Chart below. Remember, you can use this chart for any concern such as not enough money, poor health, looking for a better job etc.

Rainbow
Energy Flow Chart

A List of Emotions	B Energy Alignment
LOWEST FEELING / VIBES	
Fearful, Powerless, Despair, Desperate.	What a terrible relationship! I don't want another one. I don't want to meet anyone like that! Is there anyone out there for me? Am I ever going to find someone worth spending time with?! Yes I feel desperate to meet someone worthwhile, and yes I feel despair because everyone I meet seems totally wrong for me!
Joyless, Envious, Resentful, Grieving, Depressed.	Seeing my friends all happily married now with babies is making me envious and resentful. Another Saturday night at home on my own is going to make me totally depressed. And yes, I am grieving… if others can find someone special why can't I?
Low Self-Worth, Low Self-Confidence, Self-pity, Insecure.	What's wrong with me? Why can't I meet someone? I wish I were taller, may be I would be noticed more. Yes I am engulfed in self-pity. Of course I feel insecure after the way my last relationship ended!
Hatred, Angry, Revengeful, Distressed.	Yes I hate my ex for treating me like that. I do feel very angry about it.
Negative Self-Expression, Guilt, Aggravated, Annoyed.	Maybe I wasn't totally blameless. But if another idiot is interested in me, I'm going to punch something! They're all idiots!
Uninspired, Confused, Disappointed, Discouraged, Overwhelmed.	Oh do I want another relationship or not?! I haven't dated for so long. Just the idea is way too overwhelming. And I don't know anyone in this city. Why did I move?! I'll never meet anyone!
Unenlightened, Empty, Disinterested, Discontent.	I feel empty inside, it would be nice to be loved, and to come home to someone. If nothing else, it'd be nice to have the company. I don't want to be alone forever!

(continues)

Reverse your problem to see it as a desire. Turn your desire into a Rainbow Expression. What can you feel encouraged and hopeful about?	To find a partner who treats me with respect. We find each other irresistible. We laugh all the time and have loads in common. We want to live and have fun together.
Trusting, Encouraged, Calm, Secure, Patient.	Half my friends who were married as soon as they left college are divorced and single now anyway, so it didn't help them to rush into a relationship. Grandma and Gramps met later in life and they have the best relationship. They have been together for over 50 years now. They are still in love! That is what I want. Yes I can wait for that!
Joyful, Cheerful, Aspire, Vision, Hopeful.	Looking at my diary, I do have a lot of parties to go to. Maybe I'll meet a few nice people there?
High Self-Worth & Self-Confidence Determined, Eager.	Actually it would be superb to have a great relationship like Grandma and Gramps. Since I'm new to the area, I could join a few clubs and groups. That could be quite fun.
Love, Passionate, Certainty, Thrilled, Excited.	I love the idea of learning to dance; I'll join a jiving club. That new cafe I had lunch in yesterday is quite an active venue too; there were some really interesting people in there, and they seemed friendly enough.
Positive Self-Expression, Creative, Triumphant, Exhilarated, Enthusiastic.	I have some nice clothes and I do look pretty good. The party this Saturday should be interesting; more new people.
Inspired, Joyful Knowing, Clarity, Wonderment, Liberated	I am quite clear about the qualities I don't want anymore and those that I do want in my relationship. I am going to take the pressure off; no more hunting for a new partner!
Enlightened, Absolute Love, Total Appreciation, Pure Joy, Serene, Peaceful, Empowered, Fulfilled	I am going to have so much fun; I'll just see what happens! So my modern-day-Gramps you must be out there somewhere; come and find me!
HIGHEST FEELING / VIBES	

In this last example of changing vibes by using the Energy Flow Chart, the person's desire to meet a partner is the same, however the point of view has shifted sufficiently to be attracting rather than repelling.

Remember that the overall goal is to release the emotional blocks, which can often be caused by painful incidences experienced in your past. There are many ways in which this release can be achieved and you may already be working with someone or trying out a method that seems to be effective for you. If it feels right then that method is right for you, as it will be helping you take a Rainbow View of life.

Examples of Stepping Stones

Stepping stones are a way of giving yourself easier steps to achieve your desire. Examples are offered here to show you how to apply the idea of taking stepping stones towards your own desires.

We are all so different and what is important to one person could be irrelevant to the next. For this reason, the examples given below offer a general idea of how some people have used stepping stones to achieve their evolving desires.

Examples of Stepping Stones	
Better Health	Initial desire: To feel a little better. Picture imagine: I'm smiling more. Feeling is: relief, happy Once achieved, my next desire is: To have more time feeling comfortable. Picture imagine: I can get in and out of my chair easily. Feeling is: relief, happy Once achieved, my next desire is: To feel confident walking a few paces in comfort again. relief, happy, excited Picture imagine: My friends are celebrating with me as they watch me walk again. Feeling is: elated Once achieved, my next desire is: To be able to walk in the park again. Picture imagine: being in the park, hearing the birds, feeling the wind Feeling is: fabulous! Once achieved…to keep going with new desires and then my next desire is: To have full health again Picture imagine: Doing all the fun things I used to do. Feeling is: Fantastic!

(continues)

Greater Wealth	Initial desire: To have enough to pay my bills easily Picture imagine: For the post/mail to come and feel happy opening it Feeling is: relief Once achieved, my next desire is: having a steady source of income. Picture imagine: Seeing myself working at something I enjoy. Feeling is: proud, grateful Once achieved, my next desire is: To have money to spend on some treats knowing I can afford to buy. Once achieved…to keep going with new desires and then my next desire is: To buy a car and have a lovely home Picture imagine: Driving my new car up to my new house Feeling is: elation!
A Job / Improving current job	Initial desire: Have work that I enjoy doing, and enough time to do it in. Picture imagine: Sitting at a desk, smiling and enjoying my time Feeling is: calm, nice Once achieved, my next desire is: Having the recognition for my good work Picture imagine: My boss thanking me and giving me more interesting work Feeling is: happy, excited Once achieved…to keep going with new desires and then my next desire is: Picture imagine: Promotion Feeling is: Proud, happy
Expanding Sales Network	Initial desire: more sales Picture imagine: Filling more entries into my sales book Feeling is: relief Once achieved, my next desire is: when I call people they are in, and people call me to buy my goods and services Picture imagine: sitting at my desk, phone ringing, picking it up, another sale! Feeling is: great! Once achieved…to keep going with new desires and then my next desire is: received sales person of the month award! Picture imagine: my boss shaking my hand giving me the award Feeling is: fantastic!
New Home	Initial desire: to agree what would make up my ideal home Picture imagine: sitting over dinner having fun listing what I want Feeling is: happy Once achieved, my next desire is: to have a good, efficient agent help me Picture imagine: shaking hands with the agents Feeling is: happy Once achieved…to keep going with new desires and then my next desire is: Picture imagine: putting the key in the lock and opening my new front door Feeling is: fantastic!

Weight & Looks	Initial desire: To have my perfect weight Picture imagine: standing on the scales Feeling is: happy Once achieved, my next desire is: buy new clothes that fit easily and look good Picture imagine: looking in the mirror and loving my new clothes Feeling is: fantastic Once achieved…to keep going with new desires and then my next desire is: having new hair style, having great new clothes, great body weight Picture imagine: look in the mirror and feel fantastic outside and in Feeling is: fabulous!
Improved Relationships	Initial desire: to enjoy being with my partner again Picture imagine: laughing over dinner Feeling is: happy Once achieved, my next desire is: doing plenty of fun things together again Picture imagine: holding hands as we go out; having a great time Feeling is: happy Once achieved…to keep going with new desires and then my next desire is: going on holiday together Picture imagine: hugging, knowing that we are committed to each other and all is going to be fine Feeling is: relief, contentment
New Relationship	Initial desire: to meet someone whose company I really enjoy. Picture imagine: laughing over dinner Feeling is: happy Once achieved, my next desire is: doing plenty of fun things together Picture imagine: holding hands as we go out; having a great time Feeling is: happy Once achieved…to keep going with new desires and then my next desire is: meeting each others friends and family Picture imagine: enjoying their company. Hugging, knowing that we want to be together Feeling is: fabulous!

Notes To The Releasing Resistance Checklist

Note 1 – Am I crystal clear about what I want?

You may not be that clear about what you want. However, you need your thoughts to become clearer so that you can then focus on and achieve precisely what you want. For example, you may be saying, "I don't want to live like this anymore," or "I don't want that job anymore." Turn it around and think in general terms about the things you do want, such as to work at home more, or to work better hours.

If, for example, you no longer want to stay in your current job but you are not sure what else to do, then ask yourself loads of direct questions about the subject and decide how good your answers feel to you. For example, what hours would you like to be working… and how would that make you feel? What skills might you be using… and how would that make you feel? Keep asking yourself questions like this and jot down all the answers that make you feel good… really good. Soon, a picture will begin to evolve of what your ideal scenario would be.

This approach is applicable to any new desire; you just need to vary the questions. If you desire a new relationship, then the questions you ask relate to the various qualities of your perfect partner and how you will feel when you are with him or her. If you want to set up a new business, then your questions relate to the various products, skills and customers you would have in your perfect business scenario.

Start making a list of the various attributes and qualities you are looking for. Imagine how it would feel if everything was exactly as you want it to be and then write that down. Also try asking yourself why you want your desire, and as you come up with many, many different answers, you will begin to create a fabulous picture that will become the reality in your mind's eye of what your desire means to you.

124

Note 2 – Am I clear about what steps I should take toward achieving my desire?

In such an action-based society, we often think we should be taking some action straightaway to solve our problems. Since we tend to do this with the wrong frame of mind, things go from bad to worse. This is the reason why it is so important when you are feeling low to sidetrack your mind for a while and change your perspective so that you feel better, as this will start shifting the vibes you are sending out and the experiences you are attracting back.

Let us take an example of Paul who has just lost his job and does not have enough money to pay his next month's rent. He is highly skilled but for a specific, niche market. He is very worried that he might not be able to get another job quickly. He does not have the solution to the problem, but he knows he would feel good if he thrashed out his anger on the punch bag at the local gym. He has not been there for months. On the day that he decides to go, he meets someone and by chance they start talking. This person has a friend who has been trying for months to find someone with Paul's qualifications.

You do not need to work out where the solutions to problems will come from or how your desire is going to be fulfilled; you just need to keep heading in the right direction by changing your point of view to whatever feels best to you. As you keep your mind set on your desires, while at the same time turning your attention and doing things that feel good to you, you will be drawn to do certain things, inspired to do others and as you keep following your feel-good feelings soon you will have achieved your desires.

You can also encourage inspiration to flow in relation to what action would be good to take by asking, but not answering the question: What would be some good steps for me to take that will help me achieve my desire. As you relax, see what springs to mind. If nothing does, ask yourself the same question again later, or the next day, etc. Keep asking until something does spring to mind. Scribble down your thoughts and include any research you may have done or advice that you may have been given by others, including advice from experts. Remember that the experts are not always right and the best person to judge what is best for you is you.

When you are ready to make a decision on what action to take, try asking yourself, "Which option feels better?" If you have a few options but none of them feel good, delay taking any action and just ask yourself the same question again later. Relax and think about something else for a while. You have all the answers that you need. As your mind rests, the answer will eventually come to you. It will just feel right, and so it will have a high score on your 0-10 scale, where 0 feels terrible and 10 feels inspired. Take what action you feel is best and not what you think is best. Allow your inner wisdom to guide you by doing what you feel inspired to do.

Friends, family and experts may try to persuade you to take a different course of action than the one that feels right to you. It is fine to listen, but as long as you only do what feels best to you, then you will be moving closer to achieving your desires.

The only one who can really determine what feels best for you...is you.

If the action you are considering seems overwhelming or makes you afraid, worried, or feels like a chore, then it is the wrong action for you right now. Stop. Decide what does feel good, and do that instead. It may be that after a few moments or in a few days' time when you have had the chance to reflect on what was making you feel bad, and you look at it from a different angle, you may feel a little better. Then the same action would at that time give you the results you are looking for.

Sometimes you may wonder whether you should push yourself to do something that you have been putting off for a while. If this happens, simply remind yourself what your goals are and then ask yourself again how good does the action you are considering feel now. If you still feel that you would prefer to do something else then that is your answer.

When the action you are considering is right for you, the impulse to go ahead and do it will be very powerful.

If you are unsure about trusting your feelings, then reread the more detailed notes on Chakra One on page 28.

Note 3 - Do I really want this desire for me?

Your desire is much stronger (and therefore you are much more likely to achieve it) if you want it for yourself, rather than to please friends, family or society. If you do want your desire to please others, ask yourself why? Does the answer make you feel good or bad? For example, if you want to achieve something in order to feel good enough in someone else's eyes, then perhaps you are looking for someone else's approval, in which case you may find the Improving Your Self-Esteem Chart useful.

Note 4 - Is the desire really mine?

What if your desire is that someone else receives their desire? For example, your partner is going for a job interview and you want him to be accepted. That is really his desire, because it is his life. It is his own thoughts during the interview that will create his feelings and vibes that will determine whether he gets the job or not. You cannot think or feel for him, but you can influence your partner's vibes with your own by how you feel. Ultimately it is up to him.

If we take another example where you have a friend who is upset, the very best thing you can do in this situation is to help shift your friend's point of view, so that he can look at the situation from a different perspective.

When someone has just hit rock bottom, a gradual approach may be needed. Simply letting them know that you are there for them is a good starting point. You can then help progressively change their outlook by helping them fix their sights on a thought that is just slightly better.

Now let us take a look at the situation where your desire is to help a baby, a young child or a very old person who may not be able to understand the concepts of Surfing Rainbows. Again, you can influence what they attract into their lives by your own vibes because if you are anxious about them, they will pick up on your fear and they may feel fear as well. Conversely, if you are calm and happy, they will subconsciously pick up on that and reflect those feelings instead.

If looking at the situation in a positive light is too difficult for a child or the elder, you can help by finding something to focus on that they can feel good about. By diverting their attention in this way, you are helping them come back into balance by improving their mood. Being relaxed, calm and happy will help improve their health and whatever else they attract into their lives.

Note 5 – Am I worried about being able to handle any problems that may arise as a result of my desire being fulfilled?

What are those worries? Make a list of them.

When you have identified what your worries are, ask yourself if they are really valid and if not, can you disregard them? Ask yourself what your response would be if a friend told you they had the same desire and the same worries about it. Would you agree that the worry was valid?

If you decide that the worries are valid, turn the problems into new desires and then add them to your list of desires. For example, "I don't want to feel stressed and under time pressure all the time," this is a problem that can be turned into, "I have time to do the tasks I want to do so that I feel relaxed and cope well."

If you cannot identify what your worries are, but you are still worried whether you will be able to deal with any potential problems that may arise when your desire is achieved, you are still blocking it from materializing.

Remember that when you trust your feelings (by identifying how good or bad you feel about any topic) you will always have accurate guidance in solving any potential problems as they arise.

If you would like to, revisit the notes on Chakra One on page 28 again so that you feel safe trusting your feelings to guide you.

Note 6 - Do I have the time to allow my desire into my life now?

If you say that you want something but actually you do not feel quite ready for it, this is the vibe you will be sending out. Your feelings show the wavelength you are on and whether you are receptive to receiving your desires or whether you are blocking them from coming into your life.

Think about the desire you say you want and consider whether you feel you are really ready for it. If you feel there are other steps to achieving your desire that need to be done first, take some stepping stones. With each step that you take you come closer to achieving your end desire.

Note 7 - Do I feel safe, at this moment right now, allowing this desire into my life?

If your answer is no, or you're not sure, then ask yourself, "What are the conditions, or criteria, that I would need to have satisfied so that I do feel safe allowing my desire into my life?"

For example, you may desire to have a baby, but only under the condition that you have a loving, supportive partner who wants to help in raising your child (otherwise you may prefer not to have the baby). Likewise, you may desire to have a new home in a cleaner, friendlier neighbourhood, but only if you still have a short, easy commute (otherwise you may prefer to stay where you are for the time being).

Sometimes the actual condition you need satisfied may not be that clear to you, but if this is the case, identify what you do not want, then simply reverse it. For example, if you do not want to feel like you are under too much pressure… then you do want to cope well. Always state your condition in a positive way. In other words, rather than saying, "I don't want a long commute," instead say, "I want a short commute." For some more examples please see page 148.

Once you recognize what conditions you need to feel safe, you will not subconsciously block your desires from being drawn to you.

By stating your conditions, you are controlling the situation that you are attracting but you are not controlling the actions of others, even though you may be influencing them. This is because, as you change your own vibes, you will be evoking your desired qualities in either someone that you already know or in someone new.

Note 8 - When I think about my desire, do I hear myself saying "I can't have that because ..."?

List all the reasons why you think you cannot have your desire and then turn each of those issues and problems into new desires.

Let us take the example where the first desire reveals a second one. "I want to go on holiday... but I don't have enough money / but I don't have anyone to go with / but I'm too sick to fly." In this example, the first desire is to go on holiday and the second is to have enough money, or to have a friend to go on holiday with or to be healthy enough to actually go away.

So my new desire is to earn enough for a nice holiday etc. and I can then write that down as a new desire and go through Steps 1 and 2 in relation to that new desire.

If the reason why you do not believe that you can have your desire is because you feel it is too far out of your reach, then take a step back and take some stepping stones to it instead. For example, if you are unwell but want full health, the idea of walking to the shops may be an impossible dream for you right now. So ask yourself what you feel you believe is possible and then build on that. Each step that feels right and feels achievable is taking you closer to your end desire.

Note 9 – If my desire is achieved, what might I have to face that may bother me?

Sometimes we say we want something but use every excuse not to go after it, because if the desire is achieved, it may mean we would have to face something else that we would find even more difficult. For example: Jack joins a dating agency but has not accepted any dates because if he decides to meet up with any of these people, he is forced to make a choice and he might choose someone who may reject him.

List all the things that you may have to face when your desire is achieved. Again, you can turn the answers into new desires. When you feel ready, run through the Releasing Resistance Checklist in relation to these new desires as well.

Here are some other examples:

- Desire: I want to be well.

- Issue holding me back: No one would need to look after me and I like being looked after. My illness gives me plenty to talk about, so if I were well, then I wouldn't have much to talk about.

- New desires: I can cope looking after myself. I have plenty of things to talk about.

- Desire: I want to have money in the bank.

- Issue holding me back: I don't manage money well so I would probably give it away, or I'd feel guilty having more than my friends.

- New Desires: I learn to manage my money well and my friends (current or new) are happy for me that I have enough to pay the rent, etc.

Before you move on, double check that you do feel safe having your desire with your additional conditions. If there are any other issues that are bothering you, then repeat the exercise.

It is also worth noting that addictions are usually smokescreens; a fear-based way of hiding from problems and fears. If you are addicted to something, then ask yourself, "What would I have to face if I didn't smoke (drink / take drugs / work so much)? If the answer is that you are worried about money or concerned about your relationship, then add new items to your evolving list of desires in order to address these issues as well. Remember that you can choose a "safe place" to visit mentally when you think about these issues (see page 91).

Note 10 - Have I wanted something for a long time but not found the motivation or inspiration to go after it?

If this is the case, ask yourself: "If I achieve this desire what would I have to face?" and look at Note 9 above.

Note 11 - Do I feel good, bad or ambivalent about the situation that I am in now?

If you feel bad about your current situation, then you will be sending out negative vibes and slipping down the negative spiral and repelling your desires. Improving your mood is vital. As you pay more and more attention to the things that please you and less time chewing over the things that are upsetting you, you will spend more of your day feeling better. This means you spend more of your day heading towards your goals.

Take a moment to look at the situation you are concerned about and complete the Energy Flow Chart in relation to it. The notes you make will become useful pocket reminders for you to refer to during your day whenever you are feeling anxious about the same issue again.

Also, take the time to consider your overall situation and see how you could feel better about it by making it more fun or more manageable. Do anything that shifts your mindset to begin appreciating what you have right now.

If you find yourself dwelling on the things in your life that upset you and make you feel bad, vent those feelings fully by yourself or with an understanding friend. Make sure your aim is to release the feelings to move into a frame of mind where you can reverse the problem by stating clearly what you do want to experience from then on. Next, aim to talk and focus on the things that make you feel hopeful and happy.

It takes some will power. You have to intentionally and consistently monitor your point of view. Once you break the cycle of being caught up in what bothers you, you will start feeling better and so you will begin attracting back more of what you want, rather than more of what you do not want.

Note 12 - When asked, "Why do you have this desire?" Does the answer make you feel good, bad or ambivalent?

The easiest way of identifying how you feel is to pose yourself the question: "Why do I really desire this thing?" If you feel ambivalent, then it is quite likely that you have had the desire for a little while and you have forgotten the good reasons for having it in the first place. If this is the case, start asking yourself "Why do I want this thing? What was it that made me excited about it in the first place?" As you re-ignite those feelings and become passionate about it again, your vibes become stronger and you start attracting it faster.

If you feel jealous when you hear of someone else achieving your desire, or if the answer to the question "Why do I have this desire?" stirs a bad feeling within you, then you are repelling the desire instead of attracting it.

For example, in Simon's situation, the question "Why do I have this desire?" raises negative feelings. He wants to set up a business and win a few orders for it, but when he asks himself "Why do I have this desire?" his answer is that he does not want others to think of him as a failure. He is worried that he won't succeed and focusing on being a failure makes this the likely result.

Sometimes it seems hard to see past your current situation and keep feeling good. Many people have it in their minds that, "when I have this, or that, then I can and will be happy," In this state of mind, their desires are likely to keep eluding them.

When we do not understand that we have powerful creative control from moment to moment, we can feel so upset or desperate about achieving something that it can turn into a real struggle.

For the person who has wanted to conceive for many years... how could she possibly feel happy about the possibility of having her own child when she has had a negative diagnosis from another expert? For her, the thought of being invited to yet another of her friends' baby christenings is complete torture.

Other examples include:
- The person who longs for a partner but in the meantime endures dinner parties surrounded by loving couples. This person finds both going to

friends' weddings and unavoidably seeing couples holding hands on holidays totally devastating.

- A person in the depths of despair over not being able to afford the next rent payment and unsure of how he will pay for groceries. He always feels excruciating embarrassment when he visits friends who have large houses and are able to afford to dine in expensive restaurants.

We always attract situations and events that are a vibrational match to us. So if we worry about not having our desires, we are focusing on the "not having" of them, and we attract more of that – more of the "not having". When we let go of the struggle we come back into alignment energetically, and so we go with the flow and we are taken to our desires. This is such a vital point to grasp.

If we try to fake how we feel and just put a brave face on the problem, that does not help at all. Our vibes broadcast how we feel. If a friend tells you he is fine but you can sense that he is depressed, do you believe his words or his mood?

How can you possibly see past your current situation and feel good about it? Remember that your point of view determines where you are heading and what you are attracting into your life. If you really want to change your situation, you have to be determined to change your perspective, and that means letting go of the negative thoughts.

As a starting point, ask yourself if there is an underlying emotion to this struggle. What does it really matter if this desire is not fulfilled? What are you afraid of? Is it the fear of being abandoned, of feeling insecure or of feeling angry, etc.? (if a painful memory is triggering your limiting belief take a look at Note 23 as well).

These limiting beliefs can all be released by reversing the problems and stating them as new desires. So having clarified that there is a fundamental underlying negative emotion which needs addressing turn it into another new desire, so from identifying that the main reason for the struggle is because you feel insecure, make this into the new desire of …I feel secure now. Go through the process of releasing resistance in relation to this new desire as well.

Now we turn back to the issue at hand and address the struggle itself. How bad you feel when you struggle shows you how much you want your desire, and since what you have been doing to achieve it has not worked, then it may convince you to try this new approach.

Releasing the struggle does NOT mean becoming resigned to the situation that you are currently in, as that implies losing hope that things will ever change for the better. Letting go means you are letting go of the tension and stress surrounding your negative point of view and moving into a more relaxed and positive mindset.

In essence, struggle means feeling bad about an issue because you are focusing on not having it. By listing what you don't like about the problem at hand you can then identify what you do want instead. By clarifying your desire again, releasing resistance and using the Energy Flow Chart you can begin to feel more hopeful and happy about it again.

Remember that since you cannot feel bad when you feel good, if you take your mind totally off the issue and have some fun, and if you make a conscious decision to only consider the actual issue from a more hopeful point of view (again with the help of the Energy Flow Chart) then you will automatically begin to release the struggle. You will be raising your vibrational energy and you will begin attracting the things you do want.

It takes great determination to change your mood when something upsetting you is constantly in your line of vision, such as seeing loving couples when you want to have a relationship or experiencing back pain when you want better health or paying bills when your bank account is empty. However, you must change your mood if you want to change your situation.

However hard it may at first seem, make a commitment to yourself to take your mind off what bothers you. Place your attention onto something fun and find something to appreciate.

Change is something that you can control and be actively involved in. By consciously deciding to direct your thoughts onto what makes you happy and onto what you do appreciate in your life, you are raising your vibes. These feelings of gratitude realign your energy levels. The process of change becomes one of fulfilment.

Note 13 – When I get in a panicked, stressed state about things, do I divert my attention immediately by changing my point of view?

If you ever get that feeling of being in the middle of a massive nightmare, so full of panic that you cannot even think straight, you have to try to catch yourself before going down the negative spiral. Immediately change your outlook by doing something that takes your mind away from the problem or refocus on an aspect of the issue that is more positive.

Do anything that will slightly shift your mood. This is so very important to understand, because if you are stressed about your desire not being achieved, the desire cannot come to you. You receive back what you send out, in which case there is no point in being stressed about it. You may as well do something else anyway. When you do something else, when you relax about the problem, the desire is still there but the vibes you are sending out are totally different; they are attracting rather than repelling. When that happens you allow yourself to achieve your desire.

Note 14 – Do I always look for a better point of view?

The feelings you have about any issue have the capacity to affect other areas of your life as well, so look at all your feelings as a whole because they affect you as a whole.

For example, Mike receives some news that he perceives to be bad and so is upset and angry. He jumps into his car to go to the shops but his mind is elsewhere and he is involved in an accident. He did not consider the accident to be his fault and he is furious with the other driver's reaction, so they start arguing. It soon escalates into a punch-up and the police become involved as things become worse. By the time the police have finished their questioning, Mike has not only missed the shops but he has also missed a deadline at work. When he finally arrives home exhausted and stressed, he shouts at his partner. Another argument starts... and so on it goes.

Perhaps this example is exaggerated but it shows the beginning of a downward spiral and why letting yourself feel bad about one area of your life has the capacity to affect negatively other areas as well. It is important to acknowledge how you feel but dwelling on negative thoughts will create an imbalance in your energy levels and cause a drop in your vibrational levels. This is why looking for a more positive point of view is an effective way of minimizing the impact of difficult or stressful situations.

If you really do want your desire, it is imperative to stay determined to look for a point of view that genuinely feels better to you. If this is still unclear, or you are not convinced, you may like to revisit the notes on Chakra Two on page 33.

Note 15 - Do I believe that I can have my desire?

Ask yourself this question when you are in different moods to see if you answer it the same way every time. Ask yourself when you looking into your eyes in the mirror.

If the answer is that you do not believe you can have your wish, then give a quick, instinctive response to the question: "Why don't I believe that I can have it?"

Your response will either reveal a limiting belief that you may be able to dispel immediately, or you may have identified a new condition or criteria that needs to be attached to your main desire. Alternatively, you may have identified a new desire to add to your list of desires.

It is worth reminding yourself that if a so-called expert has said that you cannot have your desire, they may not be right. History has shown that there is always a first time for everything.

If you feel that your desire still seems overwhelming or too far out of your reach for whatever reason, then you can give yourself more manageable goals, stepping stones that you find easier to believe will take you step by step to accomplishing your end goal. For example, you may find that "making new friends and being invited to parties" is an easier first step towards the desire "I meet my soul mate."

Remember that you will only allow into your life that which you believe you can have, and so improving your feelings of self-worth are also key. You may like to revisit the notes on Chakra Three on page 36 so that you regain and maintain high self-worth.

Note 16 – Can I have this desire now, or does something else have to happen first?

If you feel something else needs to happen first, ask yourself, "What is it?" When you have identified what you feel needs to happen, it may become clear that this block is not necessarily valid after all and can be disregarded. If a friend told you that they had this same desire but could not achieve it until this other thing was achieved, what would your response be? Would you agree?

If you do decide that something else does have to be accomplished first, turn it into a new desire and Surf Rainbows for it.

You need to believe that achieving your desire is possible and within reach. You have to find a number of positive thoughts that begin to instill a belief in you that you can have what you want. To this end, you may find it useful to collect magazine pictures that depict your desire. This gives your subconscious mind evidence that if others can enjoy it... so can you! Little by little, as you look at the collection of pictures every day and dwell on the feelings of enjoying your desire as if it were already fulfilled, your subconscious point of view will gradually begin to shift and become more open to accepting and welcoming that this desire could really be a possibility for you too.

Note 17 – Can I picture myself enjoying my desire?

If you are finding it difficult to see yourself enjoying your desire, it may mean you do not really believe it is possible and so your subconscious mind will not allow it into your life. As a starting point, you may like to try the tip given in the last note, which relates to collecting pictures from magazines.

When your mind is too full of worries, try diverting your attention onto something that makes you feel a little better. Focus on anything that takes your mind away from your problem.

As you turn your attention onto something else that feels good to you, and as you begin to feel better, you will be attracting your desires to you. This is because the feeling that you will enjoy when you have your currently unfulfilled desire is the same as when you focus on things that make you happy. So, you will be attracting your desire by matching the vibrational frequency of what it would feel like to you when that new desire is fulfilled.

If you are still not sure about the impact of your feelings, then you may like to revisit the notes on Chakra Two again on page 33.

Note 18 - Do I worry about what others will think of me if I have my desire?

Are you afraid that if you achieve all that you want, your friends won't like you any more? Why is that? Are you living your life for them or for yourself? Are you limiting your own potential, lowering your self-worth and giving your power away to the opinions and reactions of others? Do those people really know you? How can they know what is best for you when they are not you?

Do they have the level of success and happiness that you want? If they do not, it is their choice and that is fine for them, but you can reach beyond that. If someone really loves you, surely they would want you to be happy. If they do not want you to be happy, then why would you place such importance on their opinions?

Do you really need their approval? It is more important to find your own approval rather than the approval of others. When you approve of yourself, you will attract others who are more likely to as well.

You do not have to shut yourself off from the people who do not have the same opinion as you. You can love someone and be happy knowing that we are all different. That is what makes life so diverse. It may be that the people you think are not supportive simply don't know how to be, or they are being supportive in their own way, even if that does not meet your own needs.

There are millions of people in the world. Do you want friends, partners or colleagues who will keep you back or help support you as you move forward?

Make a new desire or a new condition to attach to your original desire, stating that you are fulfilling your desire with the support from others. Run through the Releasing Resistance Checklist in relation to this new desire as well.

As you send out a more positive vibe, that is what you will attract back either in the people you already know, or in new friends.

Note 19 - Am I open to being loving and do I encourage good relationships?

To encourage good relationships, you first have to feel loving towards yourself. How you feel about yourself plays a large part in how you expect you will be treated. If you are unable to treat yourself with loving respect, then it is unlikely that you will treat others that way. And because like attracts like, the lower vibes attract vibes of the same level and you receive back treatment that reflects how you feel about yourself. So, you need to value and love yourself. You need to believe that you are worthy of love and to hold that love as it is fundamental to receiving love in return.

Can you tell yourself that you love yourself? If you answered yes, then are you able to lavish the same care on yourself that you would want to give to someone else? Starting with yourself is important because it is your life.

Note 20 – Do I only focus on the desire I *DO* want rather than on what I *DO NOT* want?

Whatever you give your attention to (through your thoughts, words and actions) you attract more of the same. If this comes from a positive outlook, your vibes are high and you receive positive experiences. If your outlook is negative, your vibes are low and the downward spiral takes over. This point is worth clarifying. For example, you may think you are focusing on having plenty of money when throughout your day you are worrying about not having enough of it. Consequently, you are actually focusing on the lack of money and therefore attracting more of that!

Turn your problems into desires again and run through the Releasing Resistance Checklist. You may also like to revisit the notes on Chakra Five on page 42 so that you understand why it is imperative to stay focused only on that which feels good to you.

Note 21 – Do I take time to relax a little everyday?

Allowing yourself some time-out daily in some form or another lets off steam so that any problems you come across may not seem quite so insurmountable. Making time to relax allows your inner wisdom to "speak" and thus your thoughts can be turned into inspired actions.

If you do not take time out to relax, then revisit the notes on Chakra Six on page 45 so that you remind yourself of the importance of relaxing every day and how that helps realize your desires faster.

Note 22 - Do I enjoy my day, knowing that my desires are unfolding?

If the answer to the above is no, then you may like to revisit the notes on Chakra Seven on page 48 to understand why you should be able to enjoy your day, knowing that your desires are unfolding. To remind yourself of how far you have already come on your journey to your end desire list the milestones that you have achieved, which are taking you closer and closer to your end goals. If however you have only just started out on your journey, take a look at all the other things that you have achieved in your life. Being able to acknowledge all that you have is very empowering. It is like attending an awards ceremony and each item you list is a "Well Done!" for you and helps give you more confidence that you will achieve your other desires too!

These may be things that you have completely taken for granted, such as your home, family, friends and job.

Continue to follow your feel-good feelings, and keep adjusting the direction you are heading in so that you do reach the desires you are aiming for.

Note 23 - Do I always go through the process of minimizing thoughts and memories that upset me and maximizing thoughts and memories that uplift me?

When answering the questions on the Releasing Resistance Checklist, if a memory comes to mind that triggers a hugely negative emotional response, this will be worth releasing.

Sometimes even the thought is so upsetting that you might prefer to skirt the issue rather than try to release it. However, the deep-seated negative energy that you are storing within can still be hurting you.

Negative thoughts make you sick. They literally eat away deep inside; they are poisonous to your health and to your life in general. You can lose so much energy and sleep over such situations that they cloud your thinking and taint the way you see life. The trick is not to avoid or bury the bad feelings but to release them. You do not have to release the person or situation that caused you the upset, but you do need to release the negative emotion itself. Here are a few ideas that may help, (remember that you have the choice of going into your safe place when you carry out these exercises see page 91 for more details):

1) Dig deep to see if there was an underlying feeling that was buried beneath the bad feelings around the event that upset you. Was it that you felt insecure, abandoned, disappointed, humiliated, not good enough, rejected, unloved, unable to express who you really are? If nothing immediately comes to mind, ask yourself the question later. As you turn your mind to something else, the answer will eventually come to you.

You can only truly release the deep negative feelings when you have worked out what buttons were really pushed. Releasing emotions can sometimes peel away in layers like an onion skin; the issues dealt with may reveal more negative emotions. Be glad that they are surfacing for you to identify and release. With every shift in mood as you begin to feel better, you will be increasing your energy levels.

142

Once you have an idea of what may be the underlying emotional feeling, then you can reverse this deep-seated negative emotional block into a new desire. For example, if the underlying feeling was that you felt unable to express who you are, then your new desire is to have the strength to always be yourself. When you Rainbow Express this new desire, you will then be seeing yourself with this attribute and drawing on your subconscious mind to assist you in achieving it.

The process of releasing negative emotions needs to feel safe and controlled for you to make progress and for some this can be more easily achieved if you talk to a friend or professional therapist. Once you can recall the incident without feeling bad, then it does not carry the associated negative energy. Once that is done, the rest is easier and healing can occur as you turn to release the emotional block relating to the issue itself.

2) To be sure that you are truly releasing, rising above and going beyond your deep-seated negative feelings, take another look at the emotions listed at the top of the Energy Flow Chart and use them in relation to the situation that you felt bad about. With each new emotion you dwell on, ask yourself whether there is a particular part of your body that feels tense when you think about that emotion, situation or person.

When a child is hurt, it will cry, but after a while it will turn its attention to something else, the pain is forgotten and the new focus allows it to become totally happy again. In the same way, you also need to allow yourself to fully release the bad feelings by crying, punching pillows, shouting and writing letters that you burn or tear up rather than send. Do anything to vent your feelings safely in your own space. When you have finished you will feel the relief of release.

Imagine breathing deeply and sending pure white light and positive energy to the particular part of your body that felt tense when you thought about the emotion, situation or person.

3) If you felt someone else's actions were at the core of why you feel bad, remember that if this person had your knowledge and background they may not have done what they did, but they are not you. With the knowledge and background that they had they may feel that what they did was quite

reasonable. As a quick reminder, see the example in the Allowing of Others exercise on page 94.

What is important is to have wonderful energy around you now. To achieve this you have to release the negative from past memories. So, even though it may well seem like an enormous challenge, and without having to condone what happened, try hard to find a better perspective of the person or situation.

4) Consider what possible good could have come from the situation that made you feel bad? At the very least it should help you become crystal clear about what you DO want to experience in the future and that means you can create a new desire and turn that into a Rainbow Expression. If you are having trouble trying to look at the situation in a positive light, ask yourself the question again: "What possible good could come from what has happened?" and then relax your mind and go and do some nice things. As you relax more, ask yourself the question every now and again later until the answer eventually comes to you.

5) You choose how bad you feel about a situation. You can make light of it or you can dwell on every bit of it and blow it up even larger. It is the meaning we give to situations that determines how we feel about them.

When your vibes are high and you consciously change your view on a situation, you reverse the negative impact it may have. Ask yourself what there is to love or feel good about the person or situation that you had felt bad about. If you dwell on the good parts of a relationship or situation, you are not condoning the initial action that caused you hurt, but the relationship or situation can become bigger and the problem can become smaller. Remember if you continue to feel bad about an old memory, the only person it hurts is you. So take back your power and renew the relationship with this person or the event that happened by remembering some good things about it.

As you send out a more positive vibe, that is what you will attract either in someone you already know, or in someone new.

6) Changing your perspective about the event lessens the impact of the situation. It is the importance you give to something that determines how you

feel about it. Without condoning the situation, try finding ways of changing the importance you give it, so that you are free to move on.

One method you may like to try is to reduce the event to an irrelevant cartoon in your mind. The reason for trying this out is because when you feel bad it is still negatively affecting your reality. For a brief moment, try picturing the scene where you felt bad and then make the scene black and white, instead of colour and draw some silly noses and big ears on the people concerned. Make the characters do silly things and give them oversized clothes and floppy hats. Make it funny.

Whatever you do with the image to help shift the emotional importance you give it will help free you of the negative feelings that are holding you back.

For some, turning a painful event into a cartoon will work, while for others it will not. We are all different. Keep trying different methods until you feel ambivalent about the event that had upset you.

Another method you may like to try is to find a wonderfully positive emotion that you could pepper through the scenario as you remember it. For example, consider a child that felt horribly abandoned by her parents who left her with strangers in a foreign country without being given any idea that they were coming back to pick her up. Her true emotion was to feel abandoned and that caused huge emotional blocks throughout her life until she released the pain from that childhood memory.

The method of releasing the negative memory that worked for her was to replay the scenario that triggered this emotional block over and over again in her mind, peppering it with nicer thoughts rather than just fearful thoughts.

She thought of lovely things that happened just before the incident and imagined lovely things that happened afterwards. She knew logically that her parents did not mean to upset her and so she transferred the true knowledge of this into the event itself by adding to the event things that would have made her feel safer. Some examples were that her parents would have told her that they were coming back at a certain time; that they would have given her something nice to play with while they were away and they would have made a huge loving fuss over her on their return. After adding many different aspects like this to the scenario that had upset her, she now remembers this event without any hurt or upset.

Although the additions to the event that she now recalls were not actually real, she knows the essence of the feeling was there, because they did love her and they did want her to be happy. Now when she remembers the event it does not bother her.

Different ideas will work for different people. The overall aim is to feel fine when you remember the event that bothered you.

7) If you are in the habit of reliving the pain of a negative memory then remember that when you dwell on things that make you feel bad, you feel worse. Also, remember that you do have control of what you think about.

However hard it may seem, totally absorb yourself in something else that pleases you. As you keep going over the ideas given here to help you release bad memories, you will know that you have released the negative emotional blocks by the way you feel about the issue. You will be free from the negative emotional pull of the issues that had held you back when you recall them and you will not feel bad about them.

Turning Your Desires into Rainbow Expressions

These examples are aimed at giving you a general feel of how to turn what you don't desire into focusing on what it is you do desire, and from there converting what it is you do desire into a Rainbow Expression.

How you feel about your desire and Rainbow Expression is what is most important. For example if you say that you want to be well, it is how you feel when you say these words that will determine what you are actually focusing on and what you are attracting. So if you say you want to be well but that makes you think about all your aches and pains, then it would be more effective to say, "I enjoy better and better health," so that you are focusing on just that instead.

What you don't desire...	What you do desire...
To not be so fat, so skinny, so spotty	Having my perfect weight, with clear skin and feeling great about myself.
To not always feel so bad about myself.	Discovering what I am best at and enjoy doing. Imagine myself really excelling and feeling proud.
To not always be ill	Feeling very well and doing things that I want to.
To not have everyone fighting at home	Enjoy calm and happiness at home.
Not having enough money to buy the things I want	Having enough money to buy the things I want.
To not fail my exams.	Enjoying college, having fun and doing well. (Remember that the college may not be the one you *think* it is now, so be ready to look at others as well.)
To not be unemployed anymore.	Enjoying a great job, having fun, doing well and being paid well. (Remember that the best job for you right now may not be the one you *think* it is, so be ready to look at others as well.)

Examples of Conditions for Rainbow Expressing

Examples of Conditions
I am very happy to have a loving relationship where my partner loves me just the way I am and we encourage each other to keep up with our old friends, because then I will feel so loved and that makes me feel so happy! (Note about the condition attached to this desire: the suggested focus is "being loved just the way I am" rather than "having a relationship but not compromising who I am again".)
I am very happy to have success with my business and cope well with all the issues that come up because then I can support my family doing something I love and that makes me feel so excited! (Note about the condition attached to this desire: the suggested focus is "coping well with all the issues that come up" rather than "not getting stressed or overworked".)
I am very happy to have full health and manage to keep up my energy levels because then I can go on holiday and that would be fabulous, like the old times! (Note about the condition attached to this desire: the suggested focus is "managing to keep up my energy levels" rather than "not getting tired and unwell again".)

Chapter 10

Quick Reminders

The Promise of Surfing Rainbows has revealed that the crucial link between the Law of Attraction and your chakra energy centres is your energy flow as indicated to you by how you feel. The better you feel, because of the better thoughts that you think, the more in balance your energy becomes and so the better your vibes become. The better your vibes become, the faster you attract your desires.

"*The Promise of Surfing Rainbows* is one of the most fabulous metaphors for mindfully manifesting miracles I've ever seen, instantly leading you into the flow of life. The clarity and love with which this material is presented is exemplary and startling - full, unreserved and admiring recommendation from me!" Quote by The Barefoot Doctor

"Our psychoenergetics science experiments of the past 12 years have clearly and definitively shown that, properly applied human intention to inorganic, organic and living materials, can <u>significantly</u> alter the properties of such materials and what we call 'physical reality'. Utilizing *the Promise of Surfing Rainbows* diligently as a daily affirmation with strongly focused intention can, over time, also yield such results." Quote by William A. Tiller, Ph.D.

Energy-Flow Diagram

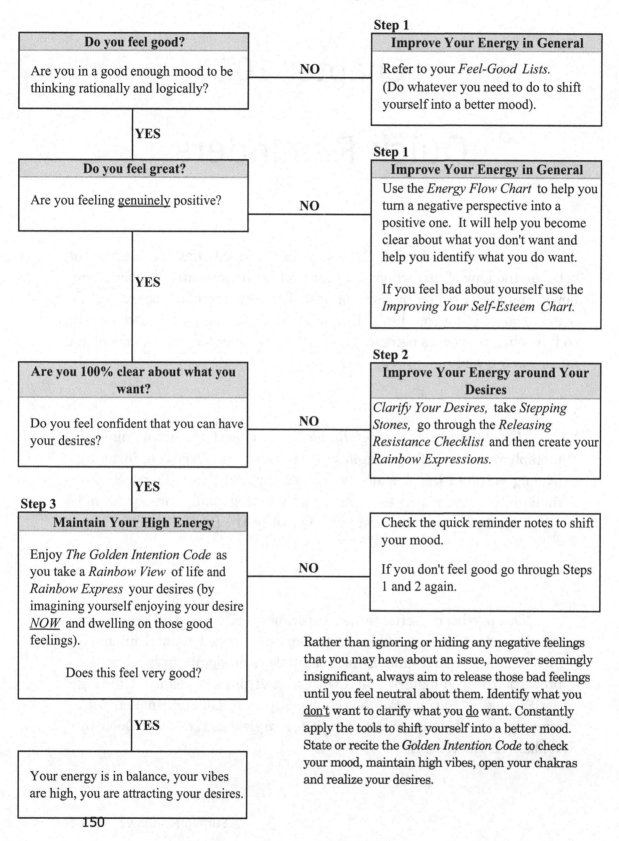

Do you feel good?

Are you in a good enough mood to be thinking rationally and logically?

NO

Step 1
Improve Your Energy in General

Refer to your *Feel-Good Lists*.
(Do whatever you need to do to shift yourself into a better mood).

YES

Do you feel great?

Are you feeling <u>genuinely</u> positive?

NO

Step 1
Improve Your Energy in General

Use the *Energy Flow Chart* to help you turn a negative perspective into a positive one. It will help you become clear about what you don't want and help you identify what you do want.

If you feel bad about yourself use the *Improving Your Self-Esteem Chart*.

YES

Are you 100% clear about what you want?

Do you feel confident that you can have your desires?

NO

Step 2
Improve Your Energy around Your Desires

Clarify Your Desires, take *Stepping Stones,* go through the *Releasing Resistance Checklist* and then create your *Rainbow Expressions.*

YES

Step 3
Maintain Your High Energy

Enjoy *The Golden Intention Code* as you take a *Rainbow View* of life and *Rainbow Express* your desires (by imagining yourself enjoying your desire <u>*NOW*</u> and dwelling on those good feelings).

Does this feel very good?

NO

Check the quick reminder notes to shift your mood.

If you don't feel good go through Steps 1 and 2 again.

Rather than ignoring or hiding any negative feelings that you may have about an issue, however seemingly insignificant, always aim to release those bad feelings until you feel neutral about them. Identify what you <u>don't</u> want to clarify what you <u>do</u> want. Constantly apply the tools to shift yourself into a better mood. State or recite the *Golden Intention Code* to check your mood, maintain high vibes, open your chakras and realize your desires.

YES

Your energy is in balance, your vibes are high, you are attracting your desires.

150

The Golden Intention Code

The Golden Intention Code Unleash Your Energy, Unleash Your Life	Chakra
I feel safe trusting my feelings to make good decisions and to guide me to achieving my desires.	1
The things in my life that make me happy are…*(think about a few of them now)*	2
Rainbow Express your desires.	2
I am unique and special. Everyone, including me, deserves to be happy and enjoy a good life. *(Reflect on something you have done ,or something about yourself that makes you feel good)*	3
The things in my life that I love are…*(think about a few of them now)*	4
I love myself. I am happy to give, receive and be surrounded by love.	4
I constantly shift and direct my thoughts, words and actions onto what feels good so that I always feel good.	5
As I relax today I welcome clarity and inspiration.	6
I enjoy my day, and the unfolding adventures of my life!	7

© 2009 Sentir

Quick Reminders

- The Golden Intention Code helps us to clearly pinpoint our bad feelings which is so very, very important. Our feelings show us when we are thinking thoughts that are making us happy or sad, and when we feel happy our chakras are more open. When our chakras are open we have higher vibes and when we have higher vibes we are benefiting more from the Law of Attraction. Therefore, our good feelings are a clear indicator that we are heading towards happy and fulfilling life experiences.

- Use The Golden Intention Code (morning and evening) to check how good you feel. If you are in a bad mood when you come to read the code then revisit the Surfing Rainbows Steps 1 and 2 or spend a moment answering a few of the questions beneath The Golden Intention Code for children on page 161 to help you feel better first.

- When you say The Golden Intention Code, the idea is not to lie to yourself, or to pretend that you do feel good, the idea is to be totally honest with yourself and to identify where you don't feel so good.

- If any part of the code doesn't feel good to you when you read it then take a look at the quick reminder notes that follow to see if that helps you feel better.

- If you understand the reasoning behind the statements of the code and want them to be true but find them hard to say, you may need some stepping stones. For example, one of the statements relating to Chakra Four is "I love myself." If you do want to love yourself but you do not feel that way yet, you can modify the statements so that you feel comfortable. In this example you could say something like, "my intention is to love myself," "day by day I am learning to love myself more" or "I treat myself with loving kindness." As your fourth chakra begins to open up more and as the days go by you will eventually feel comfortable saying what is written in the Golden Intention Code, "I love myself," and at that point, you will know that your fourth chakra is more open.

152

- Keep looking for ways to feel better and better, so that when you reread The Golden Intention Code again it does feel great and you do genuinely agree with it, so that you know you are back on track and heading for your desires again.

- Rainbow Expressing your desires: A picture paints a thousand words, so dream up new desires and make them come alive on the movie screen in your mind. Dream about them as if you have them now. Step into your movie and benefit from all those good feelings! You don't need to work out how your desires will come about. Just follow your good feelings so that they can and will come about! You may have the hunch to do this, or be inspired to take one action or another, you may meet a person that will help you in some way. All sorts of things can happen that will help you achieve your dreams.

- Remember that any bad feelings will keep your dreams out of your reach. So, if something happens in your day that makes you feel bad, decide how you would like the situation to turn out, and play that on the movie screen of your mind instead. Be determined to look for the best in everything, and take your mind off any worries by thinking about things that make you feel better.

On the following pages you will find the quick reminders relating to each statement of The Golden Intention Code and each row of questions in The Surfing Rainbows Seven Day Challenge, which will be explained in the next Chapter.

www.SurfingRainbows.com/Surfing
offers more ideas, hints, suggestions and exercises to help boost your feel-good feelings anytime during your day to help you make a habit of living by The Golden Intention Code, to keep your chakras open and your energy in balance.

Trust. Feeling secure.

The aim is to increase how safe and secure you feel during your day, so that your first chakra stays open and in balance.

The reason why it makes so much sense to trust your feelings is because they indicate whether you are thinking thoughts that are opening or closing your chakras, and so whether you are allowing greater or less energy to flow within your body…and therefore whether you are, or you are not, fully benefiting from the Law of Attraction.

Trusting your feelings simply means identifying how good or bad you feel about any topic and then using that guidance to determine your next thoughts, words and actions.

Trust your feelings to guide you because when you look for ways to make you feel good you will always feel safe.

TRY: All through your day, keep checking how good you feel. If you have an option to do a few things, ask yourself which option feels better. The option that feels best will be the best one for you at that moment in time.

For more details revisit notes on Chakra One on page 28.

Chakra Two

Joy. Feeling happy, grateful and appreciative.

The aim is to increase how happy you feel during your day, so that your second chakra stays open and in balance.

If you feel so down that nothing seems good to you, remember why you need to be determined to focus on something that will make you feel better. When you focus on thoughts that make you feel better you improve your vibes and this pulls you out of your problems and attracts you to your solutions.

TRY: By constantly focusing your attention on what makes you feel good…you will feel good. Throughout your day, make a habit of asking yourself, "What is the best thing that has happened so far today?"

For more details revisit notes on Chakra Two on page 33.

Chakra Three

High self-worth.Feeling confident and deserving.

The aim is to increase how good you feel about yourself and to keep feeling good about yourself all through your day, so that your third chakra stays open and in balance. The better you feel about yourself; the more you feel deserving of your desires and that means you welcome, expect, attract and accept them into your life. When you feel bad about yourself, you push yourself away from them instead.

TRY: Gain a stronger sense of self-worth by dwelling on aspects of yourself that you like most. Remember, every snowflake and every flower is unique and special. So are you. A flower with one petal missing is still beautiful. It is perfect with its imperfection and deserves sunlight and water. Who are we to think that the flower is not perfect or that we are not perfect, or that we don't deserve?

For more details revisit notes on Chakra Three on page 36.

Chakra Four

Love.Feeling open and loving.

The aim is to increase how open and loving you feel during your day, so that your fourth chakra stays open and in balance. This means feeling good within yourself irrespective of any negative interaction you may have with anyone else. The better you feel about others and the more loving you are, the more you will be attracting relationships and experiences that you are going to like.

TRY: Focus on the positive qualities that you like most in everyone you meet, so that you will soon be attracting more people that rate a 10 (or a 10+!) with those qualities who will enrich and support your life.

TRY: For instant, accurate feedback when you want to check how good a match someone is to you on a personal or professional basis, ask yourself how good you feel on a scale of 0-10 about the person in general.

For more details revisit notes on Chakra Four on page 39.

Chakra Five

Positive self-expression.
Feeling good.

The aim is to increase how good you feel about everything you think, say and do during your day, so that your fifth chakra stays open and in balance. If you catch yourself feeling bad, just acknowledge it, be kind on yourself and then shift your thoughts onto something else that feels better instead.

TRY: Ask yourself every now and again, "How good does this thought make me feel?" If it doesn't feel good then chose a different one!

For another reminder on why this is so important revisit notes on Chakra Five on page 42.

Chakra Six

Inspiration. Having insight and feeling inspired.

The aim is to increase how inspired you feel, so that your sixth chakra stays open and in balance.

TRY: Take time to relax and shift your mind off your troubles every day by finding other enjoyable things to do. This can be going for a walk, a leisurely bath or simply by staring out the window at the sky. Breathe deeply and allow tensions to fall away. When you release stress it naturally makes you feel better and creates a "space" in your mind for inspiration to flow.

For more details revisit notes on Chakra Six on page 45.

Enlightenment. Feeling good, enjoying the journey.

The aim is to increase how good you feel moment to moment during your day, so that your seventh chakra stays open and in balance. You can enjoy your day much more when you really understand that as long as you keep doing things that make you feel good, you are moving closer to achieving your desires because it pulls your energy more into alignment.

It is only when your energy is in alignment, because you feel good, that you are on the right wavelength to attract things that will make you feel equally good when you are enjoying them.

TRY: Become totally focused on, and enjoy whatever you are doing in every moment of your day, so that you cannot be worried about the future or upset about the past.

TRY: Add some extra fun into your day.

For more details revisit notes on Chakra Seven on page 48.

You may like to try this Golden Intention Code from The Promise of Surfing Rainbows Storybook for children. Make a fun game of it with your family and see how it lifts everyone's mood.

Here is The Golden Intention Code:

Everyone is special and I am too! When I feel great I'm heading for a life I'll love, so I look for the best in everything. I feel safe, relaxed, happy, loved and loving; loving myself and loving others. My dreams can come true and my life unfolds into a fantastic adventure!

I feel good about plenty of things in my life right now (think of a few)…and I feel great about what I see myself having…*(step into the movie screen in your mind and have fun dreaming of yourself enjoying your desires now).*

Play one of these Feel-Fab
Question and Answer Games by yourself or with your family.

In the Morning:

- What makes you smile, laugh and feel good? (think of different things)

- What's good about you? (pick different things)

- When will you have a relaxing moment today?

In the Evening:

- What was a good thing that happened today?

- What made you laugh today?

- What made you feel good about yourself today? (think of different things)

- What makes you feel most loved?

Chapter 11

The Surfing Rainbows
Seven Day Challenge

Surfing Rainbow gives you a simple and logical solution for delivering desires. To prove how effective it is, you are invited to take up The Surfing Rainbows Seven Day Challenge. As you gently shift into the open mindset that it encourages, your energy will begin to flow more freely.

Each row of The Seven Day Challenge and each statement in The Golden Intention Code focuses on enhancing the good feelings that balance each of your chakras. This will be like opening the combination lock to achieving your desires.

As you answer the questions on each row, jot down your score in the Table at the end of your day. On the right hand side of the table you will see a column for each day of the week. Every day, give yourself a score in the column provided for each of the topics mentioned. Give yourself a score based on how good you feel, where 0 means you feel bad and 10 means you feel really good.

You are invited to aim for scoring maximum points for seven full days in a row. If you have a low score on one day, start again the next until you do score full points for seven complete days in a row.

Before you see high scores in each row at the end of the day, you may have many blanks and low scores at the beginning; just remember you have another chance the next day to beat the score from the day before. See The Surfing Rainbows Seven Day Challenge as a fun yet valuable exercise to do at your own pace.

If you score less than 10 for any of the questions in the challenge, then you have shut down emotionally for some reason and that will have affected your chakras. Take a look at the relevant corresponding short notes in the Quick Reminders Chapter, and if necessary revisit steps 1 and 2 of Surfing Rainbows. Reflect on the reminder notes until the resistance has gone and you feel good about aiming for a higher score in the challenge the following day.

Before you get started, if you feel it might help you to keep going, you may like to make a list of rewards that you can give yourself every time your daily score is a little better than the day before. This may give you that extra incentive to keep going until you reach the maximum points.

The Surfing Rainbows Seven Day Challenge is a pleasure ride to your treasured desires. It is all about having fun and feeling good and helping you keep up those great feelings throughout your day so that you enjoy life more and attract more of what you want into your life.

The Surfing Rainbows
Seven Day Challenge

	M	T	W	T	F	S	S
Chakra One Trust (Feeling Safe and Secure) Did you feel safe trusting your feelings to guide you today? (If you checked 10 times how you were feeling and then acted upon this guidance so that you felt better score up to a max of 10 points).							
Chakra Two Joy (Feeling Happy) List out your desires on a piece of paper and score each of them up to 10 points depending on how good you felt about them during your day. Give yourself 10 points if you felt good all day, or if your mood dropped you improved your feelings by taking any of the Surfing Rainbows steps 1,2,3. If you Rainbow Expressed the desired outcome of your day in the morning, give yourself 10 points. If you progressively Rainbow Expressed the desired outcome of some key events during your day, give yourself another 10 points.							
Chakra Three Worthiness (Feeling Deserving) How deserving did you feel about having your desires today? How good did you feel about yourself today? (The better you felt the more points you score, up to a maximum of 10 points for each of the above two questions.) Give yourself another 10 points if you took a moment to improve how you feel about yourself by: • Accepting past compliments given to you by others. • Reflecting on anything you have done that made you feel good about yourself. • Appreciating various aspects and qualities about yourself.							

(continues)

	M	T	W	T	F	S	S
Chakra Four Love (Feeling Loving) Did you stay open and loving throughout your day? (The better you felt within yourself the more points you score, up to a maximum of 10).							
Chakra Five Positive Self-Expression (Feeling Genuinely Positive) On the whole, how good did your thoughts, words and actions make you feel today? (The better you felt, the more points you score, up to a maximum of 10).							
Chakra Six Inspiration (Feeling Inspired) If you switched off your mind and relaxed today give yourself 10 points. Have another 10 points for encouraging inspiration to flow by asking, but not answering, a question. As you relax see what springs to mind.							
Chakra Seven Enlightenment (Feeling Enlightened) If you enjoyed your day, have 10 points. If you felt like you had a fantastic day, have another 10 points.							
TOTAL = MAXIMUM = Your maximum score is 140 + 10 points for each desire.							

You can take the Challenge on your own or have some fun doing it with other Rainbow Surfers at **www.SurfingRainbows.com/Surfing**

Chapter 12

Website Workshop

Playing with infinite potential for unlimited possibilities

More uplifting ideas are offered on our website www.SurfingRainbows. com. They are offered as a way of helping you make a habit of optimizing your energy throughout your day.

You are invited to try out these uplifting ideas with the objective of continuing to help yourself balance your own energy so that you create the life you absolutely love living.

Aim to take one new uplifting idea whenever the mood takes you. Enjoy it. Make it a habit in your daily life and then move on to the next uplifting idea. Take as long as you need over each task, there is no time frame; maybe it will take a few hours, a day or a few days or months. Whatever pace works for you is perfect.

Exercises and Ideas for Balancing Chakra One

Explanation:

The emotion you feel when your first chakra is balanced is that you feel safe, secure and happy. At the root of all decisions you make is either trust or fear. When you trust your feelings to guide you, then you always feel secure because you know you are always making the best decisions.

Trusting your feelings simply means identifying how good or bad you feel about any topic.

Uplifting Ideas

Every now and again during your day check how you feel, and then look for ways that would make you feel a little better. Maybe you decide to rest for a minute, maybe you look at the flower on your table (or an inspiring picture) or maybe you just turn your attention to something else for a moment, feel better and then keep going with whatever you are doing - in a better mood. The idea of this is to become aware of your constantly changing feelings, to acknowledge and honour them by doing something to make you feel better throughout your day.

Some people think they should watch the news every day to know what is happening in the world, but have you ever questioned the ratio of positive to negative news stories reported? Plenty of wonderful things are happening in the world around us every day, yet many of these events can be overlooked by the newscasters.

During your day, start becoming aware of what drains you of energy and look for ways to change how much you hear, talk, see or eat things that drain you. Notice how everything you watch on television, hear on the radio and read in the papers makes you feel; anything that leaves you feeling depressed, angry, down, heavy, drained or low is indeed sapping your energy and affecting your chakras, thereby impacting your health and your life in general.

Exercises and Ideas for Balancing Chakra Two

Explanation:

The aim is to live a life that is filled with joy rather than sadness and disappointment.

Uplifting Ideas

You are encouraged to appreciate your world as it is right now and to feel good about what you already have. When you shift your focus from what you, and others, do not have and become more grateful for everything that you do have, this helps to encourage a mentality of abundance so that you start attracting more of what you want, rather than more of what you do not want.

For Abundant Wealth

If you would like more money, then here is a fun technique that has often been praised for giving successful results.

Put $5, $10, $20, $100 or more (or a different amount of the currency where you live) in your pocket and every so often during your day think of a whole raft of things that you can buy with that money. Every now and again you can also think of putting that money into your bank account. If you are spending a larger amount of money you may prefer to leave the money in your bank, but the whole point of the exercise is how you feel every time you consider what you *can* buy with that money or how it would pile up if you kept putting that amount into your bank account.

Remember, your point of attraction is how you feel at every precise moment during your day. The more moments that you feel good about, and the more moments you feel abundant about money, the faster you will attract more of it into your life. So jump into plenty of good-feeling moments whenever you get the chance and know that you can indeed spend that money on the different items that you like. You are not pretending because you know you have the money right there and each time you do this exercise you can indeed buy that item.

By the end of the day you could have spent your money so many times over and could have enjoyed the feeling of spending $100,000 by doing this exercise. Yes, it's true you are not actually spending it, but when you imagine yourself spending it and you feel how that feels when you have plenty of money to spend on anything that you desire, it accomplishes the same thing as actually spending it. Even though it might be true that that is all the money you have right now because the rest is debt. The more you jump into the feeling of enjoying knowing that you could buy those various things, the more you will be boosting your feeling of abundance and the faster it will arrive in your reality.

When you think and feel that you have plenty of money, you will attract plenty of money. Your point of attraction is always based on the way that you are thinking and feeling. From your place of feeling abundance, you cannot attract lack of abundance. You will only attract more abundance.

For Abundant Health
When you think and feel the joy of having good health that is what you attract. Again, your point of attraction is always based on the way that you are thinking and feeling from moment to moment throughout your day. If you want abundant health every now and again throughout your day, remember how good you felt when you did have good health. What did you do and how did it feel? Perhaps you used to walk the dog, go skiing or dancing, etc. Remember those good feelings and dwell on them. Jump into those feelings for a while, really dwell on them and bring them into the present.

Let's take the example of having a bad back that gives you agonizing pain. The idea of the abundance exercise here is to take your mind away from your bad back and to enjoy the good health that you do have in other parts of your body. You may argue that it is hard to feel the wellness of other parts of your body when you are in so much pain, but **if you want to regain full health, you need to focus on being well rather than being ill.**

Be grateful that you can see, that you can hear, that you can eat easily; there is plenty to be grateful for and appreciative of. Sometime it may seem really hard to take your mind off all your pain, but this is so important. You need to find something to do or focus on that will distract you. Try watching funny films or listening to music that you really like to distract your mind and forget about the pain for a while. The more things that you can do that take your mind off your worries, the better you will become. Think about the parts of you that enjoy good health. Be grateful that your joints work so well, for example, or that your eyesight is good and that you can hear, etc. You are not pretending; you are enjoying the good health that you really do have in other parts of your body.

The more you can shift your focus away from however ill you felt before starting this exercise and turn your attention to those parts of you that do feel good, the faster you will find that the rest of your body begins to heal itself as well.

For General Abundance

If you want a loving relationship, then every now and again throughout your day dwell on the good feelings you have from the other good relationships you enjoy, such as with friends, family members or pets, etc. The more you take your mind off what you do not have and enjoy what you do have, what you want will come to you

For more general abundance to come to you, take a moment to appreciate and be grateful for the endless supply of oxygen you breathe and the flowing water to drink and bathe in.

The idea is to put on hold the thoughts about what you do not have yet and enjoy what you do have instead.

Tables

The Surfing Rainbows Crucial Link

The Promise of Surfing Rainbows has revealed that the crucial link between the Law of Attraction and your chakra energy centres is your flow of energy as indicated to you by how you feel. The better you feel, because of the better thoughts that you think, the more in balance your energy becomes and so the better your vibes become. The better your vibes become, the faster you attract your desires.

The emotional states for successfully achieving your desires are the same as when **all** your chakras are in balance, and when this happens, the resulting emotion is that you feel good.

To enjoy the positive news
from around the world see
www.SurfingRainbows.com/Surfing

Table #1

The Surfing Rainbows Crucial Link	
Emotional state required for successfully achieving desires	Characteristics enjoyed when Chakras 1-7 are in balance
1. Trust our feelings to make good decisions to take advantage of opportunities that come our way. When this happens we feel good.	1. Trust. Safe, calm, secure, patient. With these qualities we feel good.
2. Feel happy because we have clearly identified our new desires and we are holding an optimistic perspective on them. When this happens we feel good.	2. Joy. With this quality we feel good.
3. Feel confident about ourselves and we are happy to allow our desires into our lives. When this happens we feel good.	3. High self-worth and self-confidence. With these qualities we feel good.
4. Feel open and able to sense with whom to have good relationships that may open doors to new opportunities for us. When this happens we feel good.	4. Love of self and others. With these qualities we feel good.
5. Stay optimistically focused on our target to achieve it. When this happens we feel good.	5. Positive self-expression. With this quality we feel good.
6. Feel open to receiving flashes of inspiration that help fulfill goals. When this happens we feel good.	6. Inspired. Clarity. Insight. With these qualities we feel good.
7. Enjoy life on our journey to achieving each of our desires, as our lives comprise the unfolding of our never-ending stream of desires. When this happens we feel good. Very good.	7. Enlightened to enjoy the present moment fully and this means we feel good. Very good.

Self-healing Your Body & Your Life

First, here is a quick recap of a few of the main points for those who may still have some reservations on the relevance of chakras to your energy and health.

The chakras themselves do not have any power to heal you. The chakras are like energy valves: they are simply open, closed or somewhere in between. When your chakra energy valves are in balance, you have optimum energy flowing and so you have better health. When they are closed, you have less energy flowing and you tend to become ill. Since your thoughts, which are apparent through your feelings, affect whether your chakras are open or closed, if you improve your mood by releasing the negative thoughts that cause emotional blocks and focus on thoughts that make you feel good, you begin to feel better and your health improves.

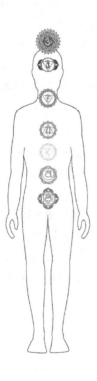 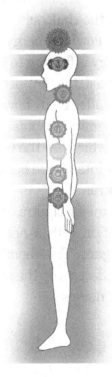

7th Chakra (purple)

6th Chakra (indigo)

5th Chakra (blue)

4th Chakra (green)

3rd Chakra (yellow)

2nd Chakra (orange)

1st Chakra (red)

The Seven Major Chakras
© Sentir 2009

Holistic therapies enjoy great success because of the results achieved. The premise of the different holistic therapies is the same: when the body is in balance (which is what happens when all your chakra valves are in balance and functioning fully) the body has sufficient energy flow to heal itself completely from physical ailments.

You can align your energy by yourself through Surfing Rainbows and you can do it with the support of your holistic practitioner. You may like to try Surfing Rainbows while being given some holistic treatment by your therapist, and then continue Surfing Rainbows between the sessions to help maintain your optimized energy flow.

For complete healing to occur, you need to address what caused the problem or disease (dis-ease) in the first place, otherwise the same, or different, symptoms simply recur. Through understanding how your feelings open or close your chakra valves and how this increases or reduces the energy flow to the different parts of your body, you can trace the symptoms within your body back to the emotional states that may have caused them. Let's reconfirm this point: the chakras themselves cannot heal or harm you. They are just a means of allowing energy into your body. What impacts your health is how much energy is flowing to the various parts of your body.

As stated, the flow of energy is affected by how balanced your chakras are and that is affected by how you think and therefore feel. Thoughts and feelings produce chemical impulses called peptides and the largest clumps of peptide receptors (which are the brain's system of communicating with the body in an effort to maintain good health) are concentrated in the locations that correspond to the chakras.

Each major chakra is linked with particular parts of the body through its association with a nerve plexus, endocrine gland, lymphatic system and various organs. The chemical hormones secreted by endocrine glands have a dramatic effect, as do the nerve transmissions within the brain, spinal cord and peripheral nerves.

If you would like greater health in any of the areas listed in columns B or C in Table 2, ask yourself if you can identify with the feeling of needing more of the qualities listed in the associated column D. Then, to make the emotional changes to bring the specific chakra back into balance, look at column E. When you start Surfing Rainbows you will be balancing all the chakras.

By understanding how your emotions affect your health and by making the decision to look for a means to feel progressively happier about everything you focus on through your thoughts, words and actions, you are taking responsibility for your health, happiness and life.

Table #2

Self- Healing Your Body & Your Life				
A **Chakra** **And associated chakra colour**	**B** **Location of this chakra** **Associated endocrine gland and bodily system**	**C** **This chakra affects the health of the following parts of the body, and the following sense**	**D** **Qualities you will feel when this chakra is in balance.**	**E** **How to bring the qualities listed in Column D into your life every day.**
1. Base / Root Red.	Base of the spine. Adrenals. Prostate gland in men. Sacral plexus Elimination, Immune and Skeletal systems.	Spinal column, kidneys, bladder, rectum, teeth and bones, legs, feet and ankles. Sense of smell.	Trust. Feel safe, calm, secure, patient, trusting and able to relax.	So that you feel more secure and calm learn to trust your feelings to guide you. This gives you access a great source of inner wisdom. The more you trust this inner wisdom the more evidence you will receive that it gives excellent guidance that will always keep you safe. For more detail see notes on Chakra One on page 28.
2. Spleen/ Sacral Orange.	Navel. Gonads. Lumbar Plexus. Reproductive system.	Sexual organs, large intestine, lower vertebrae, pelvis, kidneys, bladder, hip area and appendix. Sense of taste, appetite.	Joy. Take pleasure and appreciate others, your life experiences and yourself. Intimate, sociable.	So that your life becomes a lot more joyful focus on what makes you feel good and appreciate aspects of your life as they are right now. For more detail see notes on Chakra Two on page 33.
3. Solar Plexus. Yellow.	Solar Plexus Pancreas and Adrenal Glands. Muscular system, the skin as a system, the solar plexus, the digestive system and sympathetic nervous system.	Liver, stomach, gallbladder, spleen, the lower back, middle spine, skin, other organs and glands in the region of the solar plexus. Sense of Eyesight.	High Self-worth, Feel in control Have sufficient self-confidence and self-acceptance. Responsible, reliable and spontaneous. Feel the freedom to be oneself.	So that you have a stronger sense of self-worth dwell on aspects of yourself that you like the most. For more detail see notes on Chakra Three on page 36.

4. Heart. Green.	Centre of the chest. Thymus. Cardiac plexus. Immune and circulatory systems.	Heart, blood, lungs, bronchial tubes, upper back, skin, diaphragm, shoulders, arms and hands. Sense of touch.	Love. Love of self and others. Spontaneous with emotions. Kind, caring supportive, understanding, compassionate and friendly. Radiating a peaceful, loving uplifting energy.	To give and receive more openness and love in your life, learn to trust your feelings to guide you as this always keeps you safe and protected. This also makes it easier for you to open your heart. For more detail see notes on Chakra Four on page 39.
5. Throat. Blue.	Base of the throat. Thyroid and parathyroid glands. Respiratory system. Brachial / cervical plexus.	Throat, mouth, ears, arms, hands, neck, vocal cords, mouth, teeth and gums, jaw, ears, muscles and lungs. Sense of hearing.	Positive Communication. Creative. Positive self-expression is easy and clear, with a good sense of timing. Good listener.	To enjoy more positive self-expression focus your thoughts, words and actions on what makes you feel good. This will help you solve problems and raise your vibes to attract situations and people to you that you will like. For more detail see notes on Chakra Five on page 42.
6. Brow / Third Eye Indigo.	Centre of the forehead above the eyes. Pituitary and Pineal Glands. Carotid plexus. Autonomic nervous system.	Lower brain, left eye, ears and nose. Sixth sense, intuition.	Inspired. Clarity. Good intuition. Open-minded. Feeling of clarity.	To enjoy more flashes of inspiration and clarity in your life, learn to trust your feelings to know when to take some rest and to know what "hunches" to follow. For more detail see notes on Chakra Six on page 45.
7. Crown. Purple / White.	Top / crown of the head. Pituitary and Pineal Glands. Central nervous system, Muscular and skeletal systems.	Upper brain, right eye and skin.	Enlightenment. Wholeness. Fully integrated sense of oneness and peace with yourself and the world around you. Fully enjoy the unfolding present moment.	To enjoy a more enlightened life, trust your feelings through-out your day so that you focus on the aspects of what you are doing that please you. In this way you will be enjoying every moment of your day and attracting your never ending stream of desires. For more detail see notes on Chakra Seven on page 48.

Notes:

1. This Table does not offer medical advice, diagnoses or treatment of symptoms, although it can help to create the optimal environment in which healing has the best possibility of happening.

2. The emotional states of the lower chakras need to be in balance to fully realize the emotional states of the higher chakras.

Interestingly, the emotions that relate to the seven chakras are also recorded as the progressive states of emotions expressed by Maslow's *Hierarchy of Needs,* which is accepted by academics worldwide. Again, Maslow's *Hierarchy of Needs* states that as the lower emotions are satisfied then, the higher ones can be achieved.

But? But? But!

If any But's, What if's, and Maybe's are on your mind, then skip through these Buts! and see if any of them apply to you. You can then stop and review the corresponding notes given below the Table whenever you want to.

Table #3

But? But? But!
But the experts and my family say it's not possible! (See Note 1)
But I have had my future "read" and I have been told x,y,z? Maybe what I want is just not meant to be. Maybe it's not my fate! (See Note 2)
But I keep getting advice from so many people and I feel so confused! (See Note 3)
But I keep having doubts that all this will work! (See Note 4)
But am I not attracting more problems if I talk about them? (See Note 5)
But I can't have what I want until someone else stops (or starts) acting in a different way! I am stuck, stuck in this relationship / stuck in this job / stuck in this neighbourhood, etc! Is this asking me to be a doormat to the bad situation that I am in and just accept it?! My partner is so negative and must be attracting bad things to both of us! (See Note 6)
But I want the relationship with that specific person / to work in that specific company / to earn enough money from that specific venture, etc. That is what I want! (See Note 7)

But how do I know whether I am really doing something that will definitely mean that I am going to achieve my desires? How do I know I am doing it right? (See Note 8)
But it is all his/her fault! (See Note 9)
But how can I release the hurt, the pain, the fear? (See Note 10)
But how can I check that all my old anger and bad feelings towards others have gone? (See Note 11)
But how can I check that all my deep negative emotions in relation to other things in my life have gone? (See Note 12)
But is this suggesting that I shouldn't go to a therapist or doctor anymore? (See Note 13)
But how did I attract this bad stuff in the first place?! I don't think I am being negative. I think I am positive and I still don't have my desires! (See Note 14)
But where is my desire? I have tried this and it doesn't work! (See Note 15)
But I can't get my worries out of my mind. (See Note 16)
But my situation is so very serious this couldn't possibly help it! I have no hope! (See Note 17)
But it is so hard to do when I feel so terrible about my problem! I am scared and have good reason to be! (See Note 18)
But what about my addiction; it feels good?! (See Note 19)
But how long should I keep Surfing Rainbows? (See Note 20)
But I need it now! (See Note 21)
But I am afraid that it won't work and so I am trying to face the fear of what would happen if it doesn't work! (See Note 22)
But it is all too daunting! (See Note 23)
But it doesn't work because I have the same problems with my new (car / house / partner / friends, etc) that I had with the last one! (See Note 24)
But I hate everything about my life and I can't find anything to feel good about! (See Note 25)
But it is really hard and I want proof that it works! (See Note 26)
But why should I do that?! (See Note 27)
But I don't have the time for all this! (See Note 28)
But I can't do it indefinitely! (See Note 29)
But it all seems so complicated! (See Note 30)
But it is asking me to suspend reality! (See Note 31)
But what if it is all just nonsense? (See Note 32)
But I am busy this week; I'll do it another time! (See Note 33) But! But? (See Note 34)

While you are welcome to read all the following notes that relate to the questions above, you only need to read those that you feel are relevant to you at this time. You may also find this table useful to come back to as different concerns arise.

Note 1 – But the experts and my family say it's not possible!

So what!! What they believe is true for them, what you believe is true for you. You have read how the experts have been wrong in the past (page 30). What was once thought of as impossible is now commonplace, and there is always a first time for everything. Just look at the number of people who have achieved healthy results that even the medical experts cannot account for. Many have recovered from diseases that were once considered incurable!

You may be shown statistics on the reasons why others think that what you want is impossible. Those statistics are based on other people who did not have their energy in alignment; those statistics are irrelevant to you when you do get your energy back into alignment. If your desire relates to better health, then remember that balancing the body's energy is the core principle of all holistic therapy, which is hugely successful because of the results achieved... and with Surfing Rainbows you are doing this for yourself!

Note 2 – But I have had my future "read" and I have been told x,y,z! Maybe what I want is just not meant to be. Maybe it's just not my fate!

When you go to someone to "read" your future what happens is that they are intuitively reading the vibes you are sending out. Changing your pattern of thought will change your vibes, and this changes the direction you are heading in, your future and your fate.

Likewise, when you go to someone to read your tarot cards or stones, it is your current vibes that are attracting back the cards you pick for the person to interpret as your future life path. Changing your thoughts will change your vibes, the cards you pick, and the future that is read back to you... and the future that you will enjoy as your reality.

Note 3 – But I keep getting advice from so many people and I feel so confused!

The only person who can really determine what is right for you, is you. You will know what is right by deciding what feels good to you. You may like to revisit the notes on Chakra One on page 28.

Note 4 – But I keep having other doubts that all this will work!

Doubts attract more doubts that make you feel bad, and when you feel bad you are repelling your desires. Take your mind off your doubts by thinking of things that make you feel good and take a moment to re-read Chapter 6 to see why Surfing Rainbows is so effective.

Note 5 – But am I not attracting more problems if I talk about them?

Yes, you attract whatever you focus on. However it is fine to talk over problems as a way of accepting, acknowledging and improving how you feel. Rather than dwelling on the problem your objective needs to be to release any bad feeling that you may have and then shift your focus onto feeling better. The Energy Flow Chart is a very useful tool to help you achieve this.

Note 6 – But I can't have what I want until someone else stops (or starts) acting in a different way! I am stuck, stuck in this relationship / stuck in this job / stuck in this neighbourhood, etc! Is this asking me to be a doormat to the bad situation that I am in and just accept it?! My partner is so negative and must be attracting bad things to both of us!

Your partner cannot attract good or bad things into your experience; you are responsible for what you attract into your own life. That is up to you. You can be influenced by others if you let yourself be. If you let someone else's bad mood negatively affect you so that you slip into a bad mood as well, then you have chosen your bad mood and you have chosen that negative point of attraction. Conversely, you cannot directly change someone else's vibes either, but you can influence how they feel. Everyone has responsibility for their own life and their own happiness.

When you choose a more positive point of attraction by gradually finding things to pay attention to that pull you into a genuinely better mood, you are attracting better circumstances back. That means you are far from being a "doormat," which implies total loss of control. Instead you are regaining control of your life because of what you will be attracting into it. If you do want to change your situation (however dire it seems now), you don't need to wait for anyone or anything else; you just need to change your own vibes.

By focusing on things that make you feel progressively better, you will start attracting what you want. You won't be controlling others, but you will start controlling the situations that you are attracting to yourself. And this does influence others, in that as you change your own vibes, you evoke the required qualities in either someone you already know or in someone new.

Note 7 – But I want the relationship with that specific person / to work in that specific company / to earn enough money from that specific venture, etc. That is what I want!

When your mind is so fixed on how to solve a problem, you may be closed to better options. When you think that there is only one solution and focus totally on that, you can become afraid of it not happening. And, when you focus on not having something, of course that is what you attract. So instead, focus on the qualities and the essence of what you want from your dream relationships, your dream jobs, your dream house, etc, but don't be attached as to where or how it comes to you.

Also remember, if you concentrate on the faults of something or someone when you decide to change it, then the replacement is very likely to have the same faults, because you attract whatever you focus on. Basically, you attract people on your wavelength and repel those who are not.

Note 8 – But how do I know whether I am really doing something that will definitely mean that I am going to achieve my desires? How do I know I am doing it right?

First, ask yourself whether what you are currently doing to achieve your desire is working. If it isn't, then why not try something new, something free, something that has worked for others?

You will know when you are Surfing Rainbows because you will feel good.

Note 9 – But it is all his/her fault!

Even if you are absolutely correct in that it is all his/her fault, when you are blaming someone else, or justifying yourself, you are having negative thoughts and that simply attracts more experiences that you do not want into your life. When you rise above blaming and justifying, and look for something else to think and talk about that makes you feel genuinely better instead, you will be shifting into a higher vibration and your energy will become aligned again.

When you manage to break the chain of your negative thoughts and comments, you will be breaking the chain of past problems.

Note 10 – But how can I release the hurt, the pain, the fear?

When you have these bad feelings you feel powerless. If you continue to allow yourself to feel that way, the hurt will continue. Use the Energy Flow Chart in relation to the situation that you felt hurt by and take a look at Note 23 in the Examples & Notes for more detail on how to release deep-seated negative emotions.

Note 11 – But how can I check that all my old anger and bad feeling towards others has gone?

You can write down a list of everyone you ever felt a lot of anger / hatred / resentment or any other bad feelings towards. Take another look at the Energy Flow Chart and look at all the negative emotions at the top of the chart. Look through the various emotions and write the names of all the people you did, or still do feel those emotions towards. Take each of the people on your list in turn and imagine yourself talking over the issue with them. Then, follow the steps for releasing deep-seated emotions as already explained on page 142. The bad feelings will eventually melt away and dissolve. You will know when you are free of the negative emotions because you will feel fine about the situations and people. They won't bother you anymore.

Note 12 – But how can I check that all my deep negative emotions in relation to other things in my life have gone?

Rather than focusing too heavily to see what negativity there is, it is better to have a weekly, monthly or annual check to make sure that you feel good in relation to every area of your life. To do this, simply write down all the areas of your life such as family, friends, partner, children, job, house, money etc. and then decide how good you feel about each of them on a scale of 0-10 where

0 is terrible and 10 is fabulous. If any area of your life scores less than 10, decide how you would like to improve it. Make a Rainbow Expression and start Surfing Rainbows.

Note 13 – But is this suggesting that I shouldn't go to a therapist or doctor anymore?

The idea of Surfing Rainbows is that you do whatever feels good to you to do. If it feels good to go to a doctor or therapist, then go. If it feels good to take the advice given, then take it. The person who knows what is right for you ultimately is you. When you are aligning your energy, you are doing what a holistic therapist would be doing. They can do it for you, with you and support you, but ultimately the only person who can keep your energy in alignment to make a long term difference is you.

Note 14 – But how did I attract this bad stuff in the first place?! I don't think I am being negative. I think I am positive and I still don't have my desires!

If you feel genuinely positive, then you are attracting your desires. If you feel negative, then you aren't. Sometimes we are not aware of our negative train of thought. Whenever something negative happens to you, or whenever you feel some pain, ask yourself whether you had been thinking about something you felt bad about just beforehand. However, it is counterproductive to spend too long dwelling on what negative thoughts may have attracted a negative experience to you, because that is just more negative thinking. Know that the past is the past and your point of attraction is right *now*.

Note 15 – But where is my desire? I have tried this and it doesn't work!

When you worry about your desire and keep wondering where it is, then you are focusing on not having it and will attract more of the "not having." Take a moment to ask yourself honestly whether you believed it would work. Did you get what you expected? If you had doubts and were focusing on it not working, then it won't. It can't, because you would be sending out negative vibes and so repelling your desires.

You need to release the limiting belief that is causing the emotional block stopping you from attracting your desire by taking Steps 1,2,3 of Surfing Rainbows. Then you will realize your desires.

Note 16 – But I can't get my worries out of my mind.

Don't try to, because when you do you are focusing on them even more! Do what the Olympic Gold Medalists do who practice similar visualization techniques; they simply change what they are thinking about. Occupy your mind with other thoughts in order that you don't have the time to worry any more.

Note 17 – But my situation is so very serious this couldn't possibly help it! I have no hope!

When you have no hope and have become resigned that you can never have what you want; that is what you are attracting.

What have you got to lose by trying something new? Why not make a total commitment to focus on things, however small, that make you feel good and things that you can feel grateful about. Dwell on those good feelings and see what happens!

To help yourself move into a more hopeful place, you may like to do a little research to see if anyone else has achieved what you want. If they have, so can you. If no one else has achieved what you want, then remember that there is always a first time for everything. Be inspired by the millions of people who have been the first to achieve what others have said was impossible and is now commonplace.

As you change your mind to hold this more hopeful point of view, you are shifting your point of attraction and you will soon achieve your desire. When you feel bad your energy is out of alignment, but when you feel good your energy starts coming back to alignment. When your chakras are in balance and you have higher energy, you are sending out higher vibes and attracting what you want back.

All situations can be temporary. You can always change your mind today to choose a new picture of your future. This is critical because your energy and your vibes today determine what you are attracting to come into your future.

Note 18 – But it is so hard to do when I feel so terrible about my problem! I am scared and have good reason to be!

When you are scared or feel terrible about your problem, you are focusing on what you do not want and attracting more of it, so then yes, you do have good reason to be scared, but that is not helping you move towards a solution. If you want to attract the solution to your problem you have to focus on the solution and not the problem!

You need to be determined to take your mind away from your worries, your doubt and your pain. As you distract yourself from negative thoughts you will naturally begin to feel better and that is when you will be attracting your desires to you. This is because the feeling that you will enjoy when you have your currently unfulfilled desire is the same as when you focus on things that make you happy. So, you would be attracting your desire by matching the vibration frequency of what it would feel like to you when that new desire is fulfilled.

Note 19 – But what about my addiction; it feels good!?

Addictions are usually a means of trying to hide or escape from problems. The momentary relief does feel good, but it is not lasting. It feels a lot better to be free of the problem at the root of the addictive behaviour and this then frees the addiction itself.

The addiction gives a momentary quick-fix relief by dulling the bad feelings that would otherwise be felt if the root cause problem is faced. As your feelings are heightened when you give up an addiction, if you are still struggling with the issue that led you to start the addiction in the first place, the pain relating to the problem will feel even more challenging.

A successful approach to freeing yourself from an addiction, whether it is drink, cigarettes, work or anything else, is to discover the source of the problem and resolve that issue first by releasing the bad feelings, reversing the problems and turning them into new desires and then on to becoming new Rainbow Expressions. This refocuses your mind away from the problems and onto things that make you feel genuinely good so that you no longer have the same need for the addictive behaviour and it therefore becomes a lot easier to move on from it.

Note 20 – But how long should I keep Surfing Rainbows?

If you set out on a quest to reach something but stop in your tracks halfway, then it is unlikely that you will ever arrive. The simple answer to how long you need to surf rainbows has to be: a) for as long as you want your desire and b) until your desire is achieved.

Over forty different record companies turned down the Beatles before they received their first recording contract.

Thomas Edison made over 10,000 separate attempts before he invented the world's first light bulb.

At the age of 35 Abraham Lincoln was bankrupt, but he went on to be one of the most powerful and wealthy men of his time.

Think of when you plant a seed in the garden. There is no point worrying about whether it is growing enough. If you keep disturbing the growing plant, it will not bloom. Patience gives the seed the chance to turn into a stem, then a flower, which will later blossom. In the same way, as long as you are taking action that feels good to you, then you will get to your destination, as it is just made up of lots of little steps. The faster you get your energy in alignment, the faster you attract your desires.

Note 21 – But I need it now!

When you want to speed up the process, you are actually slowing it down, because the negative vibes from impatience are repelling your desire. Hard as it may seem, try to take your mind off your worries so that you relax, and focus on things that feel good. Your vibes will then attract good things and you will draw your desire to you much faster. The idea really is to enjoy the journey as your desires unfold.

Note 22 – But I am afraid that it won't work and so I am trying to face the fear of what would happen if it doesn't work!

Why?! When you imagine yourself in any situation, you are visualizing it and so you are attracting it! No wonder your desire is eluding you! Why would you visualize yourself with the worst case scenario when you want the best case scenario?

Aim to begin to feel fine with where you are right now. It may not be perfect, but there will be something about your life that you can appreciate right now. Dwell on anything that you can find to appreciate. Dwell on other things that happened in the past that made you feel good and make sure you complete the Energy Flow Chart and do some things from your Feel-Good Lists. Go back through the Steps 1,2,3 to keep your mind AWAY from your worries and doubts and only focus on what you do want! That means no plan B – you don't need one. Aim for what you want and only for what you want. If you have a plan B, that is what you will really be aiming for and so that is what you will attract!

Note 23 – But it is all too daunting!

Give yourself more manageable steps rather than a big leap, which may be tough for you to see in your mind's eye or for you to believe. For example, if you are ill and want to be better, rather than imagining yourself with full health straight away, see yourself being a bit better and when you have achieved that, keep going; keep seeing yourself progressively being a little better. Rainbow Express for that and that is what you will have.

Note 24 – But it doesn't work because I have the same problems with my new (car / house / partner / friends, etc) that I had with the last one!

If you spend time thinking about the problems and reasons for changing something when you are aiming for something new, you will be attracting more of the same old situation again, since you always get more of what you focus on. That is why so many people seem to keep having the same problems in relationships; they keep creating the same issues.

When you can look past the problems and feel good about any part of the situation (however small) then you can start attracting more of what you want, rather than more of what you do not want.

Note 25 – But I hate everything about my life and I can't find anything to feel good about!

You may hate your life now but if you change your perspective, you will attract to yourself a future that you will love. If you want your desire and you want a fulfilled, meaningful, happy life, then become determined to go out in

190

search of things you can admire and appreciate. That could mean going to an art gallery, immersing yourself in your favourite music, or anything else that shifts your mood. How you think and therefore feel affects your vibes and that affects what you attract back. When you feel good, your hopes and desires are realized, but when you feel bad, your fears are realized instead. The worse you feel, the worse things can become.

When you feel bad, you are being nudged to get back on track by looking around you to find something that makes you feel a little better so that you change your direction, your destination and your destiny.

Note 26 – But it is really hard and I want proof that it works!

You will have plenty of proof when you have been Surfing Rainbows properly for a while, because you will be enjoying plenty of fulfilled desires that had previously been eluding you. To bring you to the point where you are Surfing Rainbows naturally and instinctively, take The Surfing Rainbows Seven Day Challenge. Try achieving the maximum points for seven full days in a row. If you have a lower score on any one day, start again until you have achieved the maximum points for seven full days in a row.

Note 27 – But why should I do that?!

Because, as explained, the feeling that you will enjoy when you have your currently unfulfilled desire, is the same as when you focus on things that make you happy. You will be attracting your desire by matching the vibration frequency of what it will feel like to you, when that new desire is fulfilled.

Note 28 – But I don't have the time for all this!

Sometimes when we have mountains of things to do, adding one more thing may just seem too much. Take a moment now to reflect on how your life would improve if you enjoyed it more. This is what happens when you are Surfing Rainbows. With this in mind you may find it easier to gently make a start and have a go. As life begins to improve for you and you see some results you may then feel more inclined to find more time to Surf Rainbows to see even more results.

Note 29 – But I can't do it indefinitely!

Can you manage seven days? Take The Surfing Rainbows Seven Day Challenge.

Note 30 – But it all seems so complicated!

You may or may not understand in full detail how televisions and radios bring you pictures and music, but you still enjoy the benefits of them. Likewise, you may not understand why Surfing Rainbows works but you can still benefit from it.

Your natural state is to be happy. When you are happy, you have high energy. That means your chakras are more in balance and you are more fully benefiting from the Law of Attraction. So do things that make you happy; look for things in all situations that make you happy. If you cannot find anything good about a situation, then look at a different situation that does make you happy. The way to release struggle, emotional blocks and any other resistance is to focus on things that make you feel happier. When you relax, you automatically become happier, so choose more ways to relax and incorporate them into your day. Surfing Rainbows is simple, easy and powerfully effective.

Note 31 – But it is asking me to suspend reality!

No, not to suspend your reality but to improve it! The idea is not to ignore your reality but to get into the habit of always and immediately finding things to focus on that make you feel better, rather than focusing on the things that make you feel bad. This attracts more good situations to you and it therefore genuinely improves your reality. If you want a better relationship, focus on the qualities you like in your various relationships (this changes the vibes you send out and what you attract back).

If you want your back pain to go, then focus on the feeling of health that you have in the rest of your body or focus on funny films. When you are chatting with friends, focus on hopeful feelings about your health rather than exasperated feelings (this all helps you relax, which increases your energy and feeling of well being, and that helps the healing process in your back). Basically, the idea is to shift your mindset, which shifts your vibes.

Your perception is your reality.

It is a well-known fact that several witnesses to the same accident may be totally convinced that they saw different things. From where you are sitting right now, there could be a window with a view that you like on your left, and a window with a view that you do not like on your right. Both are reality but you can choose whether the reality you focus on pleases or displeases you. One will make you feel good and the other one won't.

When you choose a perception that pleases you, you will be living in more of a reality that pleases you. That results in you enjoying a better mood, which attracts better things to you.

Note 32 – But what if it is all just nonsense?

You could just have a go at Surfing Rainbows to see... and if you do it properly... well, then you will prove to yourself that it isn't nonsense and that it will deliver your desires.

Note 33 – But I am busy this week; I'll do it another time!

You'll always be busy. You may be busy doing things you don't want to do. When you have taken The Surfing Rainbows Seven Day Challenge and you are Surfing Rainbows, you will start being busy with things you do want to do instead. So embrace The Surfing Rainbows Seven Day Challenge when you feel it is the right time for you.

Note 34 – But! But?

If you justify, blame and argue for your limitations, they will stay with you and you will not be able to grow beyond them.

Just ask yourself how much you really do want your desire. Then ask yourself if you are prepared to try something new, and to try it properly. After all, it is free and it works. Have a go and see!

Inspiring Notes

Here you will find many inspiring quotes from people who have achieved their desires. These are offered to inspire you. Whether your own dreams are big or small, they are yours, they are important and they are achievable too.

Surfing Rainbows is worth...

Your Time

"The Promise of Surfing Rainbows is one of the most fabulous metaphors for mindfully manifesting miracles I've ever seen, instantly leading you into the flow of life. The clarity and love with which this material is presented is exemplary and startling - full, unreserved and admiring recommendation from me!" Quote by The Barefoot Doctor

THE BAREFOOT DOCTOR

Stephen Russell, known as The Barefoot Doctor enjoyed a mystically oriented childhood, studied Aikido, energy healing and meditation at age 11, studied yoga, Tai Chi in his late teens, the human psyche with the famous psychologist RD Laing in his early 20s, shamanism living with the Native Americans for four years in New

Photo by Robin Palmer

Mexico and acupuncture and Taoism in his mid- to late –twenties. The Barefoot Doctor now spends his time writing books, and doing workshops, seminars, talks and musical events around the world. www.BarefootDoctorGlobal.com

Your Wealth...

"Don't doubt yourself! Believe in yourself even if no one else does and you'll begin to discover who you really are and what you really want! When I started to believe in myself, I turned my life around. You can too, despite whatever is happening in your life right now. *The Promise of Surfing Rainbows* will help you find the power and passion within yourself to create a life beyond your wildest dreams."
Quote by Deirdre Bounds

DEIRDRE BOUNDS

With no commercial experience, no family history of enterprise and no money...just a pile of passion, masses of mistakes and a sense of humour, Deirdre Bounds recovered from ruinous addictions to build a company based on an idea she had in a bedsit. Within ten years she sold her ethical travel website company to a FTSE 100 company for millions of pounds. Deirdre continues to assist charities that support recovering alcoholics and addicts, and she enjoys a varied life with her loving family, husband and children. www.DeirdreBounds.com

Your Happiness...

"It's never too late to be happier than you are now. Let *The Promise of Surfing Rainbows* show you how!" Quote by Andy Hamilton.

ANDY HAMILTON

At the age of 72 he recorded his first album called "Silvershine" which became the biggest-selling UK Jazz Album of the Year. At 90 years old he received an MBE from Queen Elizabeth II for his contribution to music. And now at the age of 91 he is still giving soulful performances with his band, Andy Hamilton And The Blue Notes. www.AndyHamiltonsJazz.co.uk

Your Life...

"You may feel tested in many ways

You may doubt yourself and be tempted to give up

You must not give in, stay focused

You must stay determined when you're feeling down

You must enjoy what you do - it'll keep you feeling stronger

You must stay optimistic to achieve results

YOU WILL WIN - YOU WILL SUCCEED

Let life get better.

Let *The Promise of Surfing Rainbows* take you each step of the way"

Quote by Gary Eastwood

GARY EASTWOOD

Coming from a tough upbringing where money was tight. He inherited £100 from his granddad at the age of 14, and started up a scrap metal business at the age of 15. Some years later, his company www. lkm.org.uk is now worth over £20 million. He enjoys a full family life and competitively races GT cars as a hobby.

Your Health...

"*The Promise of Surfing Rainbows* contains many helpful ideas and information for people seeking to heal their lives and wounds." Quote by Bernie Siegel M.D.

BERNIE SIEGEL M.D.

The international best selling author of a series of books that include research on the impact of love and laughter on the immune system. He shares true stories of many so called "terminally ill" patients who have achieved remissions and cures. www.BernieSiegelMD.com

Your Career...

"Whether you are looking for a job for the first time, currently out of work, or maybe at the senior level of the corporate or legal ladder, thinking clearly is key for realizing your potential in your work life. Letting go of the blockages that get in the way of us making the most of our potential, allows us to redefine what we consider to be possible - and develop a growth mindset that will enable us to believe in our own goals.

The Promise of Surfing Rainbows will assist you in realizing your potential in your work life. It will boost your energy, drive, enthusiasm and also improve your self-confidence and self-respect, encouraging others to have more confidence, respect and belief in you too." Quote by Sophie Turner

SOPHIE TURNER

With over ten years experience as the Head of Learning and Development for two global law firms, Sophie currently provides executive coaching for partners to hone their leadership skills thereby helping them to realize the full potential of their business. Sophie@SophieTurnerPotential.com

Your Wildest Dreams...

"There are powerful ideas and strategies in *The Promise of Surfing Rainbows* on how to achieve any dream you've ever dreamed. Read, enjoy, but more than anything, be sure to apply."

Quote by Brian Jones

BRIAN JONES

First Balloonist to circumnavigate the Globe non-stop.

www.OrbiterBalloon.com

Your Interests...

"The Promise of Surfing Rainbows makes it easier than you might think to go from doubting yourself to trusting your own judgment. Trust and belief in yourself and your decisions are key ingredients for practical success in day-to-day living, the pursuit of ambitions, and overall happiness." Quote by Dawn Riley

DAWN RILEY

Dawn Riley, one of the best known sailors worldwide, was the first woman and youngest person ever to manage an entire America's Cup syndicate. She was the first American to sail in three America's Cups and two Whitbread Round the World races and was instrumental in providing community access to the sport of sailing. She is an accomplished businesswoman, community leader and youth sports advocate, author, TV commentator, speaker and committed philanthropist. www.DawnRiley.com

Your Inner brilliance...

"It's easy to give up hope and let your self-esteem spiral downwards when things seem to go wrong. But losing my sight has opened my eyes to discovering my ambitions and true potential so that I now live my life to the full. *The Promise of Surfing Rainbows* can help you to reignite the passion in yourself, your life and in achieving your own ambitions and releasing what you know to be your own true potential." Quote by Billy Baxter

BILLY BAXTER

Billy lets nothing hold him back. He is a former soldier who was blinded in service while in Bosnia. He has run marathons since becoming blind, enjoys horseback riding and he is also a motorcycle stuntman. Currently he is attending a two-year full time performing arts and drama course.

www.BlindBaxter.com (Billy reads via computer screen reader)

Remember, when things seem bad...

"When things just seem so bad, or like they can't get any worse, start surfing rainbows to let go of the anger and frustration, and to open your heart to love yourself and others so that your life CAN start to turn around." Quote by Liz Murray

LIZ MURRAY

Liz was born in the Bronx, New York, to poor, drug-addicted, HIV-positive parents. Liz Murray became homeless at 15, when her mother died of AIDS, and her father moved to a homeless shelter. Liz started school later than most and at the same time was supporting both herself and her sister. She was accepted to Harvard University in 2000, but she left in 2003 to care for her sick father. After her father died in 2006 of AIDS, she went back to Harvard and graduated with a degree in psychology in June 2009. www.HomelessToHarvard.com

204

Then step by step...

"Success can come to <u>you</u> regardless of your background or current circumstances. Where you are going has nothing to do with where you came from. I started out with absolutely nothing according to worldly standards but was able to achieve my dreams. Don't let anyone steal your dreams. Once you've read, understood and applied the concepts in *The Promise of Surfing Rainbows* you will be able to use this information to reach your dreams too." Quote by Mo Chaudry

MO CHAUDRY

Mo was unable to speak a word of English when he first arrived in England. After daily encounters with racism and being bullied, he left school with just one O-level exam pass. Because of the culture shock, coupled with the failure of his father's business, Mo vowed to himself that he would become a millionaire by the age of 30. With drive, focus and sheer determination he decided to go back to college while supporting himself as a doorman. Today he runs an empire worth £60 million and is Chairman of the UK's No. 1 water-based leisure attraction. www.WaterWorld.co.uk

Your dreams can become your reality...

"Our psychoenergetics science experiments of the past 12 years have clearly and definitively shown that, properly applied human intention to inorganic, organic and living materials, can <u>significantly</u> alter the properties of such materials and what we call 'physical reality'. Utilizing *The Promise of Surfing Rainbows* diligently as a daily affirmation with strongly focused intention can, over time, also yield such results." Quote by William A. Tiller, Ph.D.

WILLIAM A. TILLER, Ph.D

Professor Emeritus of Material Science and Engineering, Stanford University. He has been a consultant to government and industry in the fields of metallurgy and solid-state physics. He has five patents issued and he is the author of 7 books, 425 publications and 2 DVDs of which 3 books and 275 publications are in orthodox science and 4 books, 2 DVDs and 150 publications are in Psychoenergetic Science. www.Tiller.org

With A Little Help...

"The Promise of Surfing Rainbows is an inspiring workbook. It gives you the tools to change your life for the better." Quote by Mary Lambert

MARY LAMBERT

The international best-selling author on Feng Shui, the art of harnessing energy flow in the home, office and garden.

www.MaryLambertFengShui.com

Surfing Rainbows can...

Improve Your Relationships...

"Do you feel dissatisfied with any of your relationships, or are you looking for a way to improve a current relationship? If what you really want is the best relationship possible with each and every person that is in your life, or that comes into your life, then Surfing Rainbows will help you achieve exactly that. Whether it's having a fantastic relationship with your spouse, significant other, children, friends, co-workers, parents or your boss, *The Promise of Surfing Rainbows* gives you clear and simple steps to take, so that you can have the best relationships possible. These ideas are very practical, time-tested and proven." Quote by Robert Evans.

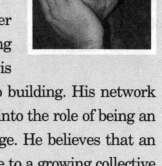

ROBERT EVANS

Robert Evans is the founder of The Messenger Network and creator of the powerful manifesting process called The Habit of Attraction. Robert is a master teacher and an expert on relationship building. His network inspires and empowers everyday people to step into the role of being an uplifting person by sharing their unique message. He believes that an expanding number of Messengers will contribute to a growing collective energy that can truly have a profound and life changing effect on our human experience. www.TheMessengerNetwork.com

Raise Your Inner Vibes...

"Our words make up less than 10% of communication, the rest is non verbal.

How we feel inside will always show on the outside through our body language.

The Promise of Surfing Rainbows is a simple, effective idea to help you shift into an all-round genuinely better mood and when this happens it has to shine through and impact positively on every aspect of your life." Quote by Carolyn

CAROLYN FINCH

Carolyn is an internationally recognized authority on speech and interpersonal communication. She is a Speech Pathologist, Kinesiologist, Color Therapist and an expert in the field of Body Language. She is also known for her extensive media appearances and corporate presentations to clients such as Mensa, Dunn and Bradstreet's Educational Services and other Fortune 500 companies. Carolyn is featured in "Who's Who of American Women," "International Professional Women," "Authorities and Experts," "Who's Who of Professional Speaking," and "Who's Who of Medicine and Health Care." www.CarolynFinch.com

Help your Inspiration to flow...

"*The Promise of Surfing Rainbows* is pure nourishment for the soul. It reminded me to take the time to step outside my life, to breathe, to look around and to let go of the stresses faced every day. In taking the time to relax, I can fully appreciate all that I do have and let the inspiration that flows through my life guide my decisions. I've remembered how to trust my own judgment and to feel proud of what I create." Quote by Diane Harvey-White

DIANE HARVEY-WHITE

Diane Harvey-White juggles the demands of being a mother of two with the pressure of running a small interior design practice. She says, 'Being a mother has taught me a lot about dealing with clients!' She constantly wonders where time goes and hopes that her children learn how to use public transport 'soon'!

And change Your World...

"Such intelligent thoughts come from *The Promise of Surfing Rainbows* to help arouse ones thinking, living and loving, even in such a way that many of the World's problems could be solved if people would apply these ideas and fill the atmosphere with calm, gentle, active energy. The whole book is very inspiring!" Quote by Dr Mary Austin

DR MARY AUSTIN

One of the first to bring acupuncture into the UK and a founding member of the British College of Acupuncture. She is also the author of the first comprehensive textbook of Chinese acupuncture in the English language.

For Your Children too ...

"*The Promise of Surfing Rainbows* is a book that can help take you from 'ordinary' to 'extraordinary.' This is an engaging, fun book that will have you 'Climbing On' to new heights in your life and experiencing life adventures you previously thought impossible. Read and enjoy this book today! You'll be glad you did." Quote by John Beede

JOHN BEEDE

Highly rated teen coach, accomplished climber and motivational speaker.
www.ClimbOnSuccess.com

The Storybook
Synopsis

. . . .

There is a version of this book for babies and toddlers that helps them to feel safe, loved, cherished and supported in their environment, while at the same time helping them to keep their chakras balanced and energy flowing at optimum levels to maintain good health. This book offers statements of intention and affirmations for children to grow up living a life they truly love.

There is also a children's version of this book called *The Promise of Surfing Rainbows Storybook*. It is a book for adults to read to children until they are old enough to read it for themselves. It is full of fun, exciting adventures to help them understand how to Rainbow Surf their way through life.

The Promise of Surfing Rainbows Storybook is a highly illustrated, enjoyable, simple read, created for children, but also enjoyed by many adults.

Indeed this book will continue to be of benefit to them as they grow up to become adults themselves, as it endeavors to capture imaginations and open minds to become more receptive to the ancient wisdom that will give them the ability to attract the very best that life has to offer.

Throughout each Chapter of the storybook synopsis, there are examples of how the thoughts and feelings that come from certain qualities referred to below in CAPITALS affect your chakras and what you attract into your life, in both positive and negative ways.

Take a light-hearted look; you may see yourself in some of the characters.

The story opens with the quest of two children who come from a family that was always struggling to make ends meet in their small flat in the city. The children had taken it upon themselves to contact the legendary singer, Sophia Rose, who had risen from the depths of poverty to reach world fame, immense wealth and popularity. It seemed a far-fetched idea at the time but John and Maggie sent the singer a letter.

They were amazed when Sophia Rose answered and invited them to visit her. When they meet the great lady, she changes their world forever by revealing to them what was behind her success... the story of Surfing Rainbows.

There have always been rainbows that appear in the sky; beautiful, coloured arcs of light that form when sunshine hits the drops of water as the rain falls.

There are other rainbows, very special rainbows, which are the home of some fascinating creatures, each of whom bears the colour of its part of the rainbow. These Rainbow Surfers, as they are called, slide down their rainbow to set out on a journey into that part of the world we cannot see, hear or touch in the usual way. Yet, we know this world exists, because these Rainbow Surfers live in each of us.

The Rainbow Surfers are taken in their LightShips on the River of Life towards The Promise at The Krystal Kavern. A LightShip automatically heads towards good experiences when its passenger feels good but turns to head towards bad experiences when its passenger feels bad. The better or worse the passenger feels, the faster the LightShip sails, whether those good or bad experiences are wanted or not!

Chapter One - Passing The NotSoSure Shop
(Chakra One – Trust)

The main character in Chapter One is Clay the Badger, who represents the first chakra, which when in balance is all about living with trust, rather than living in fear.

Clay the Badger is not keen on change; she is frightened of the unknown and therefore is often rooted to the spot, even when there is something much better just around the corner.

As the group of Rainbow Surfers set out, Clay the Badger finds it hard to let go of her fears to even begin the journey. She is so afraid to trust that she will be all right that she hides in the NotSoSure Shop. After talking with the shop assistants who put a damper on the little enthusiasm she had, she grows even more insecure and anxious about making the trip down the River of Life. Try as she might, she cannot let go of her fears.

After a disastrous beginning, Clay eventually learns how to TRUST her feelings and this gives her the confidence to step boldly towards her desires. She joins her friends as they sail off down the river towards the next jetty. From there they go inland where they follow shaded pathways until they arrive at the colourful gardens of The Parrot's Paradise.

Chapter Two - Flipping The Parrot's Coin
(Chakra Two – Joy)

The main character in Chapter Two is Sunny the Giraffe, who represents the second chakra, which when in balance is about living a life of joy rather than one of sadness.

On the way to The Parrot's Paradise, Sunny the Giraffe plods aimlessly along behind the rest of the group with his head in the clouds. He tends to wander through life, setting his sights on nothing in particular to avoid any disappointment. Iris the Butterfly encourages Sunny to raise his expectations,

214

and to let the Navigator guide his LightShip to whatever would give him JOY, as that would give his life a lot more meaning and fun.

At The Parrot's Paradise, the Rainbow Surfers are introduced to the coin tossing game between Polly the Parrot's squad and a team of Magpies. Toss a coin and only one side lands face up. Sunny the Giraffe starts to realize that it is the same with his desires; focus on what you want (the face-up side of the coin) and not on what you don't want (the down side of the coin).

Chapter Three - The Magnificent Mane
(Chakra Three – High Self-Worth)

The main character in Chapter Three is Booster the Lion, who represents the third chakra, which when in balance is all about living with a healthy sense of self-worth.

Booster the Lion has great physical strength but suffers from a lack of self-confidence because he hates the way he looks. He settles for compromise rather than reaching for his desires because he usually thinks he doesn't deserve them.

As the group of friends leave The Parrot's Paradise and go back to the jetty, they set sail once again. This time they stop-start in their LightShips and struggle to stay in a straight line with each other, learning by trial and error that any negative feelings cause their LightShips to veer off course.

When Booster the Lion found himself going round and round in circles, he shouted out, "What's going on! I've got a duff ship here!" The more annoyed he became, the more his ship took him the wrong way towards a dangerous waterfall.

At a moment of crisis it dawns on him that because of his low SELF-WORTH he has not allowed himself to have the things he wanted because he thought that he was not good enough to have them.

He begins to appreciate that he is unique and amazing just the way he is. It's at that moment that he starts to break the chains that have been holding him back.

After a dramatic rescue, he sails on with his pals to The Fabfunfairground. From there they go on to Earthrocks at The Boogie Garden, where the cool music oozes out of the stones, and the Rainbow Surfers play in some wacky sporting events.

Chapter Four - Earthrocks at Boogie Garden
(Chakra Four – Love)

Minty the Crocodile wins one of the contests. He is the main character in Chapter Four and represents the fourth chakra, which when in balance is all about living with love; loving others, loving yourself and loving your life.

Although Minty the Crocodile can be snappy when he feels defensive or over-protective, he has a heart full of love that he longs to share. As he is celebrating the fact that he won the contest, he meets a beautiful Lady Crocodile and instantly hopes to have her as a friend. Tongue-tied and shy, he is unable to talk to her. Minty's big lesson is to discover how to know if he has found a passing acquaintance, a genuinely trustworthy friend or LOVE amongst new friends.

Chapter Five - Views at Diva's Jungle
(Chakra Five – Positive Expression)

Shafts of sunlight seeped through the branches when the Rainbow Surfers left Earthrocks at Boogie Garden to go back to their LightShips. The next jetty was the stop for Diva's Jungle, which is where Chatty the Frog, who represents the fifth chakra grasps the benefits of SINCERE POSITIVE COMMUNICATION.

Usually Chatty the Frog has a lot to say, gossiping about others and chatting about all her woes and the woes of the world. However, she comes to understand that rather than focusing on, and therefore inadvertently attracting more of what she does not want, she can benefit from focusing on what she does want instead. She grasps that when she feels good about whatever she is expressing, it attracts more positive experiences back for her to enjoy, rather than more bad ones.

Chatty the Frog remembers a couple of things that Iris the Butterfly told her: "When you change how you look at something, you change how it feels to you. If you have happy thoughts, you'll experience more happiness. If you have loving thoughts, you'll experience more love, if you have healthy thoughts, you'll experience greater health and if you have angry thoughts then you'll experience more anger. Each of us sees a different world, and our world is a reflection of who we are. Change our focus and we change our world…we change *THE* World!"

Chatty the Frog realized that if she continued to think about her frustrations, then she would certainly end up becoming even more frustrated. It hit her that at every single moment she had the choice of what she could think about.

She looked up, looked left, looked right and then looked down again. Then she turned around and looked behind her. She was in exactly the same spot, but she had a new and different point of view, in more ways than one!

Chapter Six – Cocoons
(Chakra Six – Inspiration)

Later on, at The Dragonflies' Silver Grotto, where gemstone-covered silver fruit was ripe and ready for picking, Iris the Butterfly is asked about the time when she was a caterpillar. Iris represents the sixth chakra, which when in balance is about leading an inspired life.

She remembers that she never let go of her desire to become a butterfly, even though the other worms and bugs on the ground told her that her dreams were too big and she would never fly. When she was ready to make her cocoon, she never stopped loving herself just as she was, while still keeping her mind fixed on what she wanted to become… a beautiful butterfly.

She explains that when you take some time out to relax you switch *off* your mind, and so switch *on* your connection to your feelings, this is what allows INSPIRATION to flow. When it was time for her to leave her cocoon, she felt her wings lift her off the ground. It was the best feeling ever – even better than she had imagined it would be!

Chapter Seven - The Krystal Kavern!
(Chakra Seven – Enlightenment)

Pearl the Hawk is the main character in Chapter Seven. She represents the seventh chakra and is enlightened. She lives in the moment, enjoying herself on her journey to achieving each of her never-ending stream of unfolding desires.

As the friends travel to many more exotic places, they grasp that living with trust, joy, high self-worth, love and positive communication results in being inspired and enlightened. These keys to a happy life lead them to a clearing inland where they find a magnificent building with great marble towers that shine in the morning sun, and it is there that they are invited to enter The Krystal Kavern.

The Rainbow Surfers are stunned, hardly able to contain their excitement because it was at The Krystal Kavern that they discovered what they had been looking for...*The Promise of Surfing Rainbows...*

References

Books

F. Batmanghelidj, MD, *Your Body's Many Cries For Water* (Global Health Solutions, 1998).

Dr. Harold S Burr, *The Fields of Life: Our Links to the Universe* (New York, 1972).

Dr. Robert Emmons and Dr. Michael McCollough, *The Psychology of Gratitude*, 2004.

Dr. Christopher Green, *Beyond Toddlerdom*, Ebury Press (United Kingdom) 2007.

Dr. Valerie Hunt, *Infinite Mind, The Science of Human Vibrations* (Malibu Publishing, 1995).

Dr. Gregg Jacobs, *The Ancestral Mind*, (we don't have publisher information but know this is available through amazon.com)

Dr. Candace Pert, *Molecules of Emotion: Why You Feel The Way You Feel* (Simon & Shuster,1997).

Bernie Siegel, M.D., *Peace, Love, Healing* (Quill, 1998). See also Bernie Siegel's website: www. BernieSiegelMD.com

Articles In Journals & Periodicals

Abramowitz JS, Tolin DF, Street GP, "Paradoxical Effects of Thought Suppression: A Meta-Analysis of Controlled Studies," *Clinical Psychology Review.* 21(5) (2001): 683-703

"Humour Improves Health" *Brain Waves*, Society for Neuroscience, summer 2002.

Science Correspondent, *The Times* (2.9.2003), Science Editor, *The Telegraph* (22.7.2003)

Gross JJ, Levenson RW, "Emotional Suppression: Physiology, Self Report, and Expressive Behavior," *Journal of Personality and Social Psychology.* 64(6) (1993): 970-986

Roemer L, Borkovec TD. "Effects of Suppressing Thoughts About Emotional Material," *Journal of Abnormal Psychology.* 103(3) (1994): 467,474.

J.B. Moseley et al.,"A controlled trial of arthroscopic surgery for osteoarthritis of the knee," *New England Journal of Medicine*, 2002, 347:81-8.

"A meta-analysis of the association between adherence to drug therapy and mortality," *British Medical Journal*, 2006; 333:15-19

de la Fuente-Fernandez, Raul, et al., "Expectation and Dopamine Release: Mechanism of the Placebo Effect in Parkinson's Disease," *Science,* 2001;293 (5532):1164-6

Wegner, DM, Schneider DJ, Carter SR, White TL, "Paradoxical Effects of Thought Suppression," *Journal of Personality and Social Psychology.* 53(1):5-13,1987.

"Enhancing Human Performance: Issues, Theories, and Techniques," Washington DC: *National Academy Press*, 1988:274

B.Rushall, "Covert modelling as a procedure for altering an elite athlete's psychological state," *Sport Psychologist*, 1988, 2:131-140

J.A. Astin, et al., "Mind-body medicine: State of the science Implications for practice," *Journal of the American Board of Family Practitioners*, 2003; 16 (2):131-47

Van Baalen DC, et al., "Psychosocial correlates of 'spontaneous' regression of cancer." *Humane Medicine*, April 1987.

Cunningham, Alastair J., Watson, Kimberly, "How Psychological Therapy may Prolong Survival in Cancer Patients: New Evidence and a Simple Theory," *Integrative Cancer Therapies*, Vol. 3, No. 3, 214-229 (2004)

Heim ME, Köbele C., "Spontaneous Remission in Cancer," *Onkologie 1995;18:388-392*

Schwarz R, Heim M, "Psychosocial Considerations about Spontaneous Remission of Cancer," *Onkologie*, Vol. 23, No. 5, 2000.

Posted Online

Pillay, Srinivasan, *The Science of Visualization*, The Huffington Post, posted March 3, 2009

Friendly Disclaimer

The information contained in this book is intended to be educational. It does not offer medical advice, diagnosis or treatment of symptoms, although it can help create the optimal environment in which healing has the best possibility of happening. This information should not replace consultation with a competent healthcare professional. The content of this book is intended for use as an adjunct to a rational and responsible healthcare programme prescribed by a healthcare practitioner. The author and publisher are not liable for any misuse of the material.

Glossary

The Promise of Surfing Rainbows: Once you learn to Rainbow Surf through life, your deepest desires can be fulfilled. When you are Surfing Rainbows you are harnessing the powerful ancient wisdom that attracts all your desires to you.

Surfing Rainbows: Creating your life experiences by choice rather than by chance. It means that you intentionally improve your thoughts and feelings to ensure your energy flows fully to maintain a consistently high vibe and to attract your desires.

The Golden Intention Code includes:

> **Rainbow Viewing:** Balancing all the chakras to optimize your energy flow to effortlessly draw your desires to you through the Law of Attraction.

> **Rainbow Expressing:** A means of becoming clearer about your desires and intensifying your feelings about them so that you attract them faster.

> **Rainbow Energy Flow** is an abstract concept that indicates your changing moods, moving up and down the scale of positive and negative feelings. Feelings are an effective indicator as to the direction you are heading, either towards or away from your desires.

Law of Attraction. This is a commonly used term that explains the significance of our vibes. It states that the vibration we send out attracts vibrations of the same frequency back to us. Consequently, bad vibes, when we feel bad, attract our fears, but when we send out good vibes we attract good vibes back, in the form of inspiration, helpful strangers, events, "lucky" coincidences, etc., which contribute to the achieving and receiving of our desires.

Chakras. The chakras are very similar to the meridian system used in acupuncture, in that they are invisible to the naked eye. They are also similar in that they relate to specific areas within the body and when stimulated, they allow the body's energy to regain alignment. The chakras spin in a way that is similar to other fluid vortices such as whirlpools, waterspouts and hurricanes, drawing energy into them.

Crucial Link. The crucial link between the Law of Attraction and your chakra energy centres is your level of energy as indicated to you by how you feel. The better you feel, because of the better thoughts that you think, the more in balance your energy becomes and so the better your vibes become. The better your vibes become, the faster you attract your desires.

Energy Alignment. When you are feeling low and upset about an issue, aim to look for an emotion a little higher up the Energy Flow Chart that you could possibly consider appropriate. Aim to keep gradually moving up in this way so that eventually you *genuinely* feel a lot happier about it.

Your LightShip is an abstract concept in *The Promise of Surfing Rainbows Storybook* that shows the importance of feelings and energy flow.

Parrot's Coin: The two faces of a desire; one side is the desire while the other is the sense that the desire will not be fulfilled; having vs. lacking.

Flipping the Parrot's Coin: "Flipping" your anxious thoughts about your unfulfilled desire to joyful anticipation that your desire is being fulfilled; it is aligning your energy in relation to your desire. This changes the vibes you are sending out about your desire from low to high and this helps you benefit from the Law of Attraction so that your desire can be fulfilled.

The Navigator represents a great Source of Wisdom, which has been given different names by different people. It is connected to you through your feelings.

YOUR **Feelings** are spontaneous reactions to your thoughts. When you have a thought that gives you a negative feeling, this is your Navigator's guidance indicating to you that the thought you are thinking is taking you off course. If you change your thoughts to something that feels better, you will start heading in the direction that attracts your desires to you.

Rainbow Surfers: Expressions of the chakras within the body. They are:

Clay the Badger – First or Root Chakra – represents Trust/Fear

Sunny the Giraffe – Second or Sacral Chakra – represents Joy/Sadness

Booster the Lion – Third or Solar Plexus Chakra – represents High/Low Self-worth

Minty the Crocodile – Fourth or Heart Chakra – represents Love/Hate

Chatty the Frog – Fifth or Throat Chakra – represents Positive/Negative Expression.

Iris the Butterfly – Sixth or Brow Chakra – represents Inspiration/Lack of Inspiration

Pearl the Hawk – Seventh or Crown Chakra – represents Enlightenment/Lack of Enlightenment.

The Crucial Link

It was about six years ago when two people who otherwise had nothing in common met on a bus and struck up a conversation. One was a young English woman who wanted nothing more than to start a family of her own. The other was a successful American businessman who was soon to become a grandfather for the second time.

They were from very different worlds. They began a conversation that has lasted for six years over thousands of miles. The dialogue was about Life and the result is The Promise of Surfing Rainbows.

Both of them had read all the self-help books they could lay their hands on. As they shared information with each other, it became clear to them that as wonderful and helpful as those books had been, there might be something missing. They set about finding what that "something" could be and that was the gist of their trans-Atlantic phone conversations over the years.

After much discussion, trial and error, more reading and more experiments they pin-pointed what is now being called, The Crucial Link. Once that happened, and they applied the information to their lives, everything changed for them. The American gentleman saw his business grow and prosper and his children and grandchildren became happy and successful. The English woman, who had been longing to conceive for many, many years, is now the proud "Mum" of two beautiful children.

Since they had been so successful using this information, it only seemed right to share it, which resulted in them writing three books, one for babies and toddlers, one for children and one for adults.

P.D.M. Dolce is a pseudo name for the co-authors. These authors have experienced the power of *Surfing Rainbows*, as the technique came to be called, and have therefore seen their lives significantly changed for the better.

"P" had been trying for years to have a baby. By applying the principles of Surfing Rainbows, a beautiful little girl was born, followed a year later by a wonderful baby boy. It is she who created the adventures of the enchanted creatures known as the Rainbow Surfers for the children's storybook *The Promise of Surfing Rainbows* as a way of showing children and their parents how to create happy, fulfilling lives for themselves.

"D" is a businessman who has used the principles to great success in his work. However, he doesn't restrict their use to his business; he applies them to every aspect of his life and enjoys what seem to be miracles over and over again. "D" has jointly contributed to the strong philosophy that supports every aspect of Surfing Rainbows.

And then there is **"M"** who is the editor. What began as a job became a labour of love for her when she realized the value the books would hold for everyone who reads them.

Finally, there have been numerous friends who have played a part in bringing this project to you. Considerable input has been given by "S" and another "D" in their time, effort and fabulous creative talent.

We hope that you have enjoyed this book. Please do visit our website www. SurfingRainbows.com for more information. You will also see testimonials there and we invite you to add your own.

From our website you can link into a growing online environment. Over time, this will include expanded text on Surfing Rainbows, audio and video clips and an interactive journal. Access to this additional resource from our website is free and easy.

Do you know someone who you feel could benefit from
The Promise of Surfing Rainbows?

This pass-along page can be cut out and given to friends.

A promise is not something to be taken lightly. If some area of your life is not as good as you would like it to be, *The Promise of Surfing Rainbows* gives you a way to overcome any issue or issues that you might be facing. This book holds a promise that it will give you the tools that can take you to a life that you will truly love living.

Please visit our website www.SurfingRainbows.com for more information.

Do you know someone who you feel could benefit from
The Promise of Surfing Rainbows?

This pass-along page can be cut out and given to friends.

A promise is not something to be taken lightly. If some area of your life is not as good as you would like it to be, *The Promise of Surfing Rainbows* gives you a way to overcome any issue or issues that you might be facing. This book holds a promise that it will give you the tools that can take you to a life that you will truly love living.
Please visit our website www.SurfingRainbows.com for more information.